OPERATION STARLITE

*The Beginning of the Blood Debt
in Vietnam, August 1965*

Also by Otto J. Lehrack

No Shining Armor:
The Marines at War in Vietnam

OPERATION STARLITE

*The Beginning of the Blood Debt
in Vietnam, August 1965*

Otto J. Lehrack

CASEMATE
Philadelphia & Oxford

First published as *The First Battle* by Casemate Publishers in 2004.

This edition published in the United States of America and Great Britain in 2019 by
CASEMATE PUBLISHERS
1950 Lawrence Road, Havertown, PA 19083, USA
and
The Old Music Hall, 106–108 Cowley Road, Oxford OX4 1JE, UK

Paperback Edition: ISBN 978-1-61200-801-1

A CIP record for this book is available from the British Library

Typeset and design by Savas Publishing & Consulting Group

Printed and bound in the United States of America

For a complete list of Casemate titles, please contact:

CASEMATE PUBLISHERS (US)
Telephone (610) 853-9131
Fax (610) 853-9146
Email: casemate@casematepublishers.com
www.casematepublishers.com

CASEMATE PUBLISHERS (UK)
Telephone (01865) 241249
Email: casemate-uk@casematepublishers.co.uk
www.casematepublishers.co.uk

For Margaret Ann, the *sine qua non* of my life,
and for Pierrette, *mon amour*

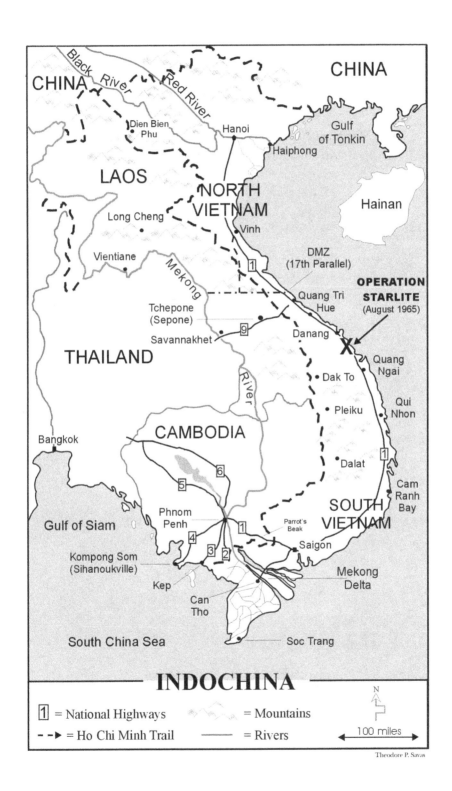

CHINA

Black River

Red River

CHINA

Dien Bien
Phu

Hanoi

Gulf
of Tonkin

Haiphong

LAOS

NORTH
VIETNAM

Hainan

Long Cheng

Vinh

Vientiane

Mekong

1

DMZ
(17th Parallel)

OPERATION
STARLITE
(August 1965)

Tchepone
(Sepone)

Quang Tri
Hue

Savannakhet

9

Danang

X

Quang
Ngai

THAILAND

River

Dak To

Pleiku

Qui
Nhon

CAMBODIA

Bangkok

6

Dalat

1

5

Cam
Ranh
Bay

Gulf of Siam

Phnom
Penh

1

Parrot's
Beak

SOUTH
VIETNAM

4

Kompong Som
(Sihanoukville)

3 2

Saigon

Kep

Mekong
Delta

Can
Tho

South China Sea

Soc Trang

INDOCHINA

N

1 = National Highways

= Mountains

- - ▶ = Ho Chi Minh Trail

= Rivers

100 miles

Theodore P. Savas

CONTENTS

Maps

Illustrations

LESSONS LEARNED

During the summer of 1965, I was deployed with a Force Recon Platoon attached to BLT 2/6 in the Caribbean, and on a particularly long patrol. The BLT Commander (there were no MEU's in those days) sent a message to all widely scattered units directing that we reveal our positions, stop action, and await his arrival. For a young lieutenant on his fourth deployment, this was as serious as it got. Rumors flew, and I recall how my Marines were convinced we were being recalled in order to be shipped directly to the country most could not yet pronounce: Vietnam. We were going to war and we were elated.

However, the scenario didn't play out that way. The cause of this remarkable pause of an entire operation was the C.O.'s intent to go to every single unit and explain firsthand the tremendous success our brethren had just brought about on a far off battlefield in Vietnam.

While greatly motivated, we were also silently disappointed we would not, as we had supposed, soon be on our way to join them.

Otto J. Lehrack's *Operation Starlite* is a graphic account of the first major clash of the Vietnam War. On August 18, 1965, regiment fought regiment on the Van Tuong Peninsula near the new Marine base at Chu Lai. On the U.S. side were three battalions of Marines under the command of Colonel Oscar Peatross, a hero from two previous wars. His opponent was the 1st Viet Cong Regiment, led by Nguyen Dinh Trong, a veteran of many fights against the French and South Vietnamese. Codenamed *Operation Starlite*, the battle was a resounding success for the Marines. Its result was cause for great optimism about America's future in Vietnam. The brutal and hot fight (both figuratively and literally) shocked the enemy as to what they could expect from Marines. With full reliance on fire support, artillery fire from Chu Lai air base north of the battlefield, naval gunfire (including an 8″ gun cruiser), and constant fixed wing air support and tactical lift by helos, the enemy experienced for the first time what Marines brought to a fight. *Starlite* set the tone for what followed. In the unlikely event the Viet Cong could ever field an independent regiment after this, it would surely never enter a fight against Marines unless fully supported by the North Vietnamese regulars.

Several months later the American Army fought its first large scale battle in the Central Highlands at LZ X-Ray (as told in the book *We Were Soldiers Once, and Young*, by Harold G. Moore and Joseph L. Galloway). This battle was fought exclusively against NVA regulars (no Viet Cong took part). However, postwar interviews revealed the NVA changed their tactics to meet the Americans in this battle because of what had been learned during the *Operation Starlite* engagement.

For those expecting a book about Americans in battle, you will not be disappointed by the detailed descriptions of how the fighting unfolded. Lehrack interviewed Marines from private to colonel during his research for this book. The battle is presented from the mud level by those who looked the enemy in the face. But *Operation Starlite* is not just another war story told exclusively from the American point of view. In researching the book, Lehrack walked the battlefield and spoke with the men who fought with the 1st Viet Cong Regiment. All of them were accomplished combat veterans years before the U.S. entered the war.

Lehrack plants his readers squarely in 1965 America—the year that truly began the U.S.'s long involvement in Indochina. Hardly anyone was against the war in 1965. Casualties numbered in the hundreds. The administration and the public thought it a noble little war in the continuing struggle against the Red Menace, and that it would be concluded quickly and cheaply. *Operation Starlite* propelled the Vietnam War into the headlines across the nation and into the minds of Americans, where it took up residence for more than a decade. *Starlite* was the first step in Vietnam becoming America's Tar Baby; the more she struggled to find a solution, the more difficult it became.

The subtitle of the book is *The Beginning of the Blood Debt in Vietnam, August 1965*. Blood debt—in Vietnamese *han tu*—means revenge, debt of honor, or blood owed for blood spilled. The Blood Debt came into Vietnamese usage early in the war with the U.S. With this battle, the Johnson Administration began compiling its own Blood Debt, this one to the American people. It was a fateful conundrum. Before *Starlite*, the Blood Debt to the American public was relatively low and relatively easy to write off. As this debit grew, Johnson and his successors came to resemble losing gamblers. They continued throwing lives and treasure into the game, hoping somehow their fortunes would reverse and the Blood Debt would be justified.

Operation Starlite also examines the ongoing conflict between the U.S. Army and the Marines about the way the war was fought. With decades of experience with insurrection and rebellion, the Marines were institutionally oriented to base the struggle on pacification of the population. The Army, on the other hand, having largely trained to meet the Soviet Army on the plains of Germany, opted to search and destroy main force units. The history of the Vietnam War is decorated with many "what ifs." This may be the biggest of them.

A year later most of the men of the platoon who had heard the Starlite message from the BLT Commander would themselves be in Vietnam. Most would return again to Vietnam; several would never return home. Each of them, however, was influenced by this battle that set the stage for long years ahead while forcing the enemy to change his intent of dominating the population areas while telegraphing the eventual downfall of the Viet Cong as an independent military organization capable of open, large scale battle with American units.

Colonel John Ripley
Director, Marine Corps Historical Division

THE TRUMPET SOUNDS

Chulai, Vietnam
16 August 1965. Afternoon.
Major Andy Comer

At about 1330 on August 16, 1965, Maj Andy Comer, the executive officer of the 3d Battalion, 3d Marine Regiment (3/3), was summoned by his commander LtCol Joe Muir, to the 4th Marine Regiment command post at Chulai. Muir told Comer that the amphibious assault on the Van Tuong peninsula, which they had frequently discussed and partially planned for, was to be executed. The 3d Battalion, 3d Marines, would make a landing from the sea while LtCol Joseph R. "Bull" Fisher's 2d Battalion, 4th Marines (2/4), would be inserted inland by helicopter. The operation was Top Secret, and information was passed out in hushed tones and on a strict need-to-know basis.

When Capt Cal Morris, the commander of Mike Company, 3/3, was called into Lieutenant Colonel Muir's tent to be briefed on his company's role in the operation, he was admonished to not even tell his company officers their mission or destination.

16 August 1965. Evening.
Colonel Oscar F. Peatross

The commander of the landing force, Col Oscar F. "Peat" Peatross, worked the Marine units all night long to get the operation up and going. About midnight, he sent his logistics officer, Maj Floyd Johnson, out to talk to Capt William R. McKinney, United States Navy, who would be the commodore of the amphibious component of the operation, to tell him to hold his ships, because at that very moment some of them were about to leave for Hong Kong. One ship had already departed and another was up in Danang to unload elements from the 9th Marines just in from Okinawa. The commodore said to Johnson, "Now this is an unusual way to run an operation. In all of my career, I've never heard of an operation run this way before." Johnson replied, "I got it direct from Colonel Peatross, who got it direct from General Walt. We're going to use your ships, and you'll get some sort of [written] directive for the operation later on." McKinney agreed and set his commanders and staff in motion.

16 August 1965. Evening.
Corporal Bob Collins

Corporal Collins was on the U.S. Naval Base at Subic Bay in the Philippines when the call came. His unit, the 3d Battalion, 7th Marines, (3/7), was on liberty. Collins had just finished eating dinner at the enlisted club with his Filipina girlfriend and was walking to the base theater to see a movie when he heard trucks with loudspeakers mounted on them calling for all 3/7 Marines to return to their ships. Collins quickly took his girlfriend to the main gate, signed her out, and went back to the ship, wondering what all the fuss was about.

16 August 1965. Afternoon.

Secrecy was the watchword. From the very beginning until all the units were underway, the Marines operated by word-of-mouth, and even then details were given to only a select few. Because the operation was so hush-hush, nothing was put to paper, and the operation wasn't named until word of it reached the 3d Marine Division headquarters. Once the division staff was briefed by Colonel Peatross's officers, Col Don Wyckoff, the operations officer for the 3d Marine Division, picked the name Satellite. He did so for two reasons: because NASA was about to launch a Gemini spacecraft the same week as the operation, and because of the unusual manner in which two battalions from different regiments, 3/3 and 2/4, would be "satellites" of the 7th Marines headquarters during the operation. As the clerks labored late into the night typing the official orders, a generator failed, and the chore was finished by candlelight. In the shadowy bunker a clerk misread the handwritten instructions and typed in "Starlite" instead of Satellite. It has often been mistakenly spelled as "Starlight" by the press, and even in some official accounts.

16 August 1965. Afternoon.
Gunnery Sergeant Ed Garr

Over in 2/4, GySgt Ed Garr figured this was not to be an ordinary operation, so he dug out a brown army-issue T-shirt that he had worn on a previous operation and which he considered to be lucky. Marines who have seen a lot of combat can be very superstitious, and many will wear favored gear or go through certain rituals when they figure something big is in the offing.

17 August 1965. Morning.
Lieutenant Burt Hinson

On August 17, 1965, Lt Burt Hinson got word from Capt Jay Doub, the skipper of Kilo Company, 3/3, to meet him at the battalion command post. Hinson was about two-and-a-half miles away. The terrain was soft sand, and being a mere lieutenant and without transportation, he was forced to hoof it, cursing Doub all the way. Once he got there, and because of the secrecy involved, Doub simply told Hinson that he wanted his platoon at the beach at a certain coordinate at a certain time, ready to board ship early that afternoon. Then he sent the lieutenant walking back across the sand once more, swearing at every step. Hinson had a love-hate relationship with Doub. "Jay Doub and I had a chemical dislike for each other. But he was the toughest man I ever met... tougher than a boiled owl." And . . . "If I ever had to go into combat again, I would like to go with Jay Doub. If there was one person I modeled myself after later in my career, it was Jay Doub."

17 August 1965. Early Evening.
Lieutenant Colonel Lloyd Childers

Lieutenant Colonel Childers and his pilots sat through a sketchy briefing about the operation. Helicopters from two squadrons were to support the initial insertion of 2/4 into the battle. The second squadron was to leave for other commitments after that, so the brunt of helicopter support was to be borne by Childers's Marine Medium Helicopter Squadron-361 (HMM-361). It was a squadron new to Vietnam but long in élan.

Colonel Childers was a U.S. Navy veteran of the Battle of Midway in World War II. He had been a tail gunner on one of two TBD torpedo bombers that had remained out of thirty-six TBDs launched against the Japanese during the battle. When his plane was fatally damaged, too, the pilot ditched the aircraft next to a U.S. Navy destroyer. Childers was badly wounded and barely conscious. Machine-gun bullets had ripped through both legs. Childers had been dragged first into a whaleboat, and then onto the destroyer, where the ship's doctor operated on him atop the dining table in the officers' mess. He was told he would never fly again. Nevertheless, by 1965 he commanded a Marine helicopter squadron and was widely regarded as an absolutely fearless and inspiring warrior. His squadron pilots and crews were proud of their daring and skill.

PROLOGUE

AMERICA 1965

For more than three decades America's war in Vietnam has been characterized as a tragedy. It was an event that tore apart the country, felled a presidency, and changed America's view of herself and the opinion of others about America. Almost no one born after the late 1940s remembers when the Vietnam War was regarded as a noble little war with scant promise of bursting the bounds of control and bearing tragic consequences.

It has almost been lost from memory that, in the late summer of 1965, the Vietnam War was not unpopular either with the American public or with the men who fought it. The men were nearly all young Baby Boomers, the sons of those who remembered the Great Depression. The Cold War and containment of communism framed the circumstances in which they were raised and which formed their beliefs. Most young males of this period expected to be drafted, or to volunteer, and to serve in their country's uniform. Their fathers had won World War II and their grandfathers had fought the War to End All Wars. It was their turn to face down evil wherever and in whatever form it appeared, and they did not shrink from the task. Having eradicated fascism in Europe and Asia, America was needed by the world to deal with the Red Menace. And an America that was just emerging from its chrysalis of innocence believed it was equal to the task. We had confidence in our government and our armed forces. We had yet to learn that democracy is not an ideology easily exported to a country where *our* indigenous high priests were avaricious and corrupt while the other side's, regardless of their political beliefs, were ascetic and nationalistic.

Moreover, at least to those who paid attention to such things, Vietnam had entertained us since the French defeat at Dien Bien Phu in 1954. It was, after all, a small, quaint, tropical country with elephants and tigers, diminutive citizens in colorful dress, and—since the rather puzzling and fatal departure of our ally, President Ngo Dinh Diem, in November 1963—a land of rotating governments. We marveled at the fiery suicides of Buddhist monks, who all seemed to be named Thich something or other; and we wondered at the evil of the crafty Viet Cong, those barefoot, slightly built peasants who could surely be beaten with just a bit of American firepower and technology. True, the French lost to them, but who, these days, were the French? They had not seemed to amount to anything since the distant high tide of the Napoleonic Wars, and France certainly wasn't the United States.

By the spring of 1965 it was clear that American firepower and technology required *Americans* to apply it, so the first regular U.S. ground troops landed. By August of that year their numbers had grown from a couple of battalions to 88,000 men. Casualties were relatively few, but their rate and frequency were escalating. Since the beginning of our involvement in Vietnam in 1959, some 906 Americans had died there. For the families and friends of those nine hundred six, each death was a tragedy. For the rest of us, casualties were not yet important. No one in his darkest dream foresaw the day when more than fifty eight thousand names would adorn a black wall in our nation's capital. Mostly men, these were the names of America's sons, husbands, and fathers. Eight million of our young men and women would serve in our nation's uniform over the next decade, and five million of these would serve in Vietnam itself, in the skies over Vietnam, or in vessels offshore. It was to pass that all of us would be affected, one way or another, by events in this tiny, far-away country.

In August 1965 this was all in the future. America was far different then. Vietnam competed with other events for space on the front pages. The cities were in their late-summer doldrums, vacations were coming to an end, and schools were preparing to open. Headlines most often dealt with domestic matters. In mid-month the Watts section of Los Angeles erupted in flames as rioting "negroes" protested their lack of civil rights. Astronauts Gordon Cooper and Charles Conrad prepared for and went into orbit in the Gemini 5 spacecraft, paving the way for Neil Armstrong to set foot on the moon four years later. *The Sandpiper,* with Richard Burton and Elizabeth Taylor, was showing at theaters across the country; the Beatles were singing for *Help;* Petula Clark was wailing about *Downtown;* and Sam the Sham was doing the *Wooly Bully.* In baseball, the Twins and Dodgers were leading their leagues and would meet in the World Series two months later. An average daily record of 6.2 million shares was traded on the New York Stock Exchange, where the Dow Jones Industrial Average had just broken 900.

Yes, Vietnam was there, all right, but it was in the shadows. For America it was a noble little war in which the depraved enemy would soon give up in the face of just, perhaps, a bit more American might, and justice would prevail in yet another place in the world. None of our crystal-ball gazers knew that Vietnam and America were at a turning point. It was in this month, in this year, that Vietnam began its advance to the foreground of our national consciousness, where it was to take up residence and remain for a decade. Operation Starlite was the first event in that journey.

Otto J. Lehrack

CHAPTER 1

INCHING TOWARD THE ABYSS

The United States came to this pass in baby steps, characterized more by Cold War fears, hubris, and inattention than by level-headed policy examination. The Soviet Union, China and, lately, Cuba, occupied the attention of planners at the White House, the Pentagon and in Foggy Bottom. For the twenty years since the end of World War II the thinkers in Washington had bigger fish to fry; Vietnam was little more than a footnote among the larger events of the Cold War. Very few American policy makers had even a vague understanding of Vietnam, its history, and recent events there. And those who did know anything about Indochina found their voices drowned by the choruses of Cold Warriors who kept the dangers of the Soviet Union and China at the head of the agenda.

The Vietnamese had been itching for self-rule for decades, and their patriotic movements gained speed and strength during World War II. After the defeat of the French Army by Hitler's Wermacht in the early days of World War II, the pro-Nazi Vichy government agreed to joint rule by the Japanese of the French colony of Indochina. Vietnamese guerrillas fought the Japanese during the Pacific War with the assistance of the American Office of Strategic Services (OSS), the proto-Central Intelligence Agency. A handful of Americans advised and fought side-by-side with Vietnamese against the common foe. The arms and training America provided were a boost to the fledgling Vietnamese guerrilla forces that would later take on the French *and* the Americans.

After the defeat of Japan in 1945, Communist Party leader Ho Chi Minh hoped to leverage his country's role against the Japanese into independence from post-war recolonization by France. He appealed to President Harry Truman to make Vietnam an American protectorate along the Philippines model.[1] Ho was a charismatic intellectual who was widely read and traveled. He had lived in New York, where in 1918 he wrote a pamphlet about appalling conditions among the Italians in Harlem; and in Paris, where, in 1920, he became a founding member of the French Communist Party. But it was not just Ho's political beliefs that led to the rejection of his proposal to the United States. The major piece of the equation was French President Charles DeGaulle's desire to regain France's former colonies. France, after all, was a major American ally, and De Gaulle's vision of a French renaissance in Asia, to say nothing of his promised assistance in Cold War Europe, won the day with the American president. The seeds of American involvement in Vietnam were planted in the little-noticed recognition of French ambitions in Indochina. A handful of years later, these seeds germinated as Cold War anxieties prompted the Eisenhower Administration to provide the French with arms and financial assistance in their war against the Vietnamese communists. By 1950 the American taxpayer was footing the bill for 80 percent of the war's costs. Few Americans knew or cared that millions of U.S. dollars were going to help the French. A debt not written in the blood of our young men is a debt easily ignored or forgiven.

The French, however, had internal problems as a result of the war. The people were suffering from casualty fatigue. World War II was not that far behind them, and the growing numbers of killed and wounded in both Algeria and Indochina fanned the flames of public discontent. The French government attempted to attenuate mounting criticism by using pro-French natives and the French Foreign Legion to bear the brunt of the struggle in Southeast Asia. This policy bought but little time. The average French citizen had had enough of bloodshed and wanted the war to end. This was a sentiment reflected fifteen years later in the United States, when American citizens brought intolerable pressure to bear on the Johnson, Nixon, and Ford administrations.

France's short-lived and sad epilogue in Indochina collapsed in 1954 at the siege of Dien Bien Phu. The French actually sought this battle. The whole reason for establishing the garrison at Dien Bien Phu was to draw the Vietnamese into a set-piece contest, which the French thought they would surely win. Dien Bien Phu was strong and it was occupied by the best French troops in Indochina. They underestimated the determination of the Vietnamese. Vietnamese General Vo Nguyen Giap's Viet Minh[2] reduced the fortified French position piece by piece with human-wave tactics, massed artillery fire, even siege works. The artillery fire came from guns hauled by hand, under conditions of extreme hardship, into the mountains surrounding the stronghold. Under unrelenting barrages of artillery fire, the Vietnamese attacked again and again until all thirteen thousand defenders were killed or captured. This was a major military and psychological defeat for the French at the hands of an army that began as a single twenty-four man platoon a mere decade earlier. The French public had had enough.

In the treaty that ended the war and dictated France's withdrawal, Vietnam was "temporarily" partitioned. The agreement also called for a general election within all of Vietnam in 1956 to determine under what sort of government the country would be unified. The Emperor Bao Dai appointed Ngo Dinh Diem to head a Western-style government in the south while Ho Chi Minh's forces took over the northern portion of the country.

Diem and Ho, like most Vietnamese, longed for the ultimate unification of their country, but each was determined to see that the unification took place under his own brand of government. Each side immediately began efforts to undermine the government of the other. The Americans, who had fought the communists in Korea and were well into the Cold War, wasted no time in shoring up the government of the southern, non-communist, half of the country under President Diem. Diem was an educated westernized Catholic and a member of the old social elite that ruled a country whose citizens were largely ancestor worshippers or Buddhists in religion and peasants by occupation. Supporting Diem seemed at the time an easy and bloodless way for America to contain communism in Southeast Asia.

Diem and his family were corrupt and more interested in maintaining personal power than in turning the country into a democracy. In November 1963 unrest among the population shook the foundations of government and the Viet Cong guerrillas, southerners who wanted to liberate the South Vietnam from Diem, threatened to take over the country. A coup led by South Vietnamese Marines removed Diem from office with American acquiescence. Hours later he and his hated brother were murdered by those who had plotted against them.

A period of coup and counter-coup followed. Policy makers in the United States, still enamored with the idea of a cheap defense against Asian communism talked themselves into supporting one general after another as each boarded the Ferris wheel of power, rode to his own brief apogee, and came to ground in yet another chapter of the continuing power struggle. There were nine different governments in South Vietnam between November 1963 and February 1965.

The chaos brought on by the tumultuous days of revolving governments opened doors for increased activity by communist insurgents in the south at the same it hobbled the effectiveness of the Saigon government. The United States, sensitive to the fragility of its South Vietnamese ally and frustrated in its inability to control events in the south, began action against the north instead.

In February 1964, the United States and South Vietnamese initiated OPLAN 34A, a series of clandestine measures against North Vietnam, including sabotage and commando raids against military installations along the coast. Although South Vietnamese conducted the actual raids, they were planned and supported by the United States. The U.S. Navy also began Operation DeSoto, sea patrols in the Tonkin Gulf. The dominant thinking was that if the Americans and South Vietnamese punished the north a little, the communists would stop their activities in the south. This naive notion persisted for years despite the lack of any evidence that the North Vietnamese and Viet Cong would give in to this type of pressure. The Americans were looking for an excuse to do more when the so-called Tonkin Gulf incident of August 1964 provided it.[3]

Assistance for the South Vietnam military persisted, first in the form of equipment, and then with advisors and yet more equipment. American casualties in Vietnam began with the deaths of Maj Dale Buis and MSgt Chester Ovnand on July 8, 1959. The two U.S. Air Force special intelligence personnel were watching a movie when a Viet Cong hurled an explosive charge into the room in which they were relaxing. For the next six years the butcher's bill slowly grew and then, almost imperceptibly, accelerated. In ones and twos at first, and then in larger numbers, the flow of body bags from Southeast Asia increased.

The U.S. Army general in charge, Paul D. Harkins, began his tenure as the Commander, U.S. Military Assistance Command Vietnam (COMUSMACV), in 1962. Harkins looked and talked like a successful general, and he was always over-brimming with optimism about the course of the war in Vietnam. Those who got out of Saigon and went into the field did not share his confidence. Among those who did go to the field were members of a new generation of American journalists who felt determined to report what they saw. These journalists—Homer Bigart, Neal Sheehan, and David Halberstam among them—became increasingly vocal about what they perceived as the real course of the war and the weaknesses of the Army of the Republic of Vietnam (ARVN). At about this time, too, many of the junior American officers in the field, where they served as advisors to the ARVN, warned of impending crises due to the inadequacies of their hosts, particularly the Vietnamese officer corps.[4] Gradually, it became evident to the Johnson Administration that something in Vietnam was wrong, so General Harkins was quietly retired and replaced by General William C. Westmoreland, U.S. Army.

Lewis Sorley, in his penetrating biography of General Harold K. Johnson, chief of staff of the United States Army from 1964 to 1968, offers some interesting observations about the appointment of Westmoreland. Sorley makes the point that Generals Johnson, Creighton Abrams (who was eventually to be Westmoreland's successor), and Bruce Palmer (who relieved General Johnson as the Army deputy chief of staff for operations) all understood the key task in an insurgency environment was to mobilize the population. Westmoreland himself, according to Sorley, did not.[5] His training, and therefore his thinking, was oriented around set-piece warfare with the Soviet Army on the plains of Germany. The names of all four generals were submitted to President Lyndon Johnson as possible successors to the discredited Harkins. Westmoreland was a protégé of Gen Maxwell Taylor, at this time U.S. Ambassador to Vietnam, and Sorely believes it was Taylor's influence that led to Westmoreland's appointment as COMUSMACV.

Having made their choice, the Commander-in-Chief, the Secretary of Defense, and the Joint Chiefs of Staff gave Westmoreland a free hand as to the conduct of the war for the next four years.[6] It was a period in which the war would evolve from a fight against pajama-clad guerrillas into one against a uniformed and well-equipped foe, one of the best infantry forces in the world, the regular North Vietnamese Army

(NVA). The NVA was an army, it should be noted, that retained an important guerrilla element: It did not fight set-piece battles; it operated in an insurgency mode.

Westmoreland's tenure was also the period in which the war would lose its popularity, or at least its acceptability, with the American public and lead to the destruction of a presidency.

It may or may not be that the newly appointed American commander in Vietnam was well grounded in the requirements of warfare in an insurgency environment. But his opponents, the Vietnamese communists, understood them very well. Their countrymen had spent centuries in opposition to invaders and occupiers.

THE ENEMY

Douglas Pike, a distinguished scholar of Indochina, calls the Vietnamese the "Prussians of Asia."[7] "The alarums and excursions of war echo like an endless drumroll down the corridor of Vietnamese history. In vast and rhythmic cycles the Vietnamese experience for two thousand years has been invasion, siege, occupation, rebellion—interspersed with lesser moments of dissidence, covert militant opposition, and other forms of social sabotage. Mentally, the Vietnamese have always lived in an armed camp."[8]

For most of its history, Vietnam has struggled to resist foreign occupation. A unique and thriving civilization that was known as Nam Viet had been in existence for several hundred years, and was a kingdom under a regent named Choa To when, in 111 B.C., the Chinese Han Dynasty sent an expeditionary corps southward and conquered it. For a thousand years the Vietnamese struggled to free themselves from the yoke of Chinese domination. During this millennium, patriots by the score made their way into the pantheon of Vietnam's heroes and achieved national status. Every Vietnamese school child knows their names. In the First Century it was the Trung sisters, who led a rebellion against the might of the Chinese Empire. Their insurrection was overwhelmed and crushed in A.D. 43, but it lasted for three years against Asia's most formidable military force. In the Sixth Century, Ly Bi took back part of the country from the Chinese, made himself king, and reigned for six years. In the Seventh,

Eighth, and Ninth centuries, Vietnamese rebellions continually rocked the southern borders of the Tang Dynasty. Finally, in the Tenth Century, Ngo Quyen freed the Vietnamese from a millennium of foreign domination when he sank the Chinese fleet at the battle of Bach Dang. Three hundred years later the Vietnamese twice defeated the Mongols, conquerors of the Eurasian continent from the Pacific shores to central Russia. Tran Hung Dao, victor in the twelve-year war against these daring horsemen, is credited with being the progenitor of the type of warfare that his successors would wage against the French and the Americans. He conserved his strength while taking advantages of the enemy's weaknesses. He always sought the support of the population. He did not try to hold territory but willingly evacuated towns, and he even evacuated the capital when necessary. He avoided combat when the enemy was too strong, resorted to guerrilla harassment, and took the offensive whenever the circumstances were favorable.

> The enemy relies on numbers. To oppose the long with the short—therein lies our skill. If the enemy makes a violent rush forward, like fire and tempest, it is easy to defeat him. But if he shows patience, like the silkworm nibbling at the mulberry leaf, if he proceeds without haste, refrains from pillaging, and does not seek a quick victory, then we must choose the best generals and defensive tactics, as in a chess game. The army must be united and of one mind, like father and son. It is essential to treat the people with humanity, so as to strike deep roots and ensure a lasting base.

In the Fifteenth Century, it was Le Loi who ejected China once more following yet another invasion and twenty years of exploitive rule. Nearly every Vietnamese city today has a Le Loi street or a statue of the great hero, or both.[9]

In the Nineteenth Century the Vietnamese met another invader against whom they struggled for nearly a century to expel. This time it was the French. The new intruder captured Danang in 1858 and laid siege to Saigon in 1859. Quickly driven back from Saigon, they returned two years later to stay. By 1883 France completely controlled all of Vietnam, and in 1887 they formed the French Union in Indo-China, which by 1893 included five regions in Southeast Asia. In addition to the three Vietnamese states of Tonkin, Annam, and Cochin China, the new union incorporated the neighboring countries of Cambodia and Laos.[10]

The French administration of the country was extremely repressive. Archimedes Patti, an American OSS officer who served in Vietnam during World War II, summed it up: "I confirmed in my reports that French colonialism in Indochina had been one of the worst possible examples of peonage, disregard for human rights and French cupidity and that for more than three-quarters of a century, the Vietnamese had been cruelly exploited, brutally maltreated, and generally used as French chattel. . . . The socioeconomic conditions generated by the French colonial system fostered discontent and rebellion. . . . "[11]

Discontent and rebellion there were in abundance and they were fueled by French practices. "French Indochina" was prescribed as the proper designation for the country and the very use of the name Vietnam was considered revolutionary and therefore forbidden. High taxes impoverished many small farmers and resulted in the concentration of land in fewer and fewer hands. Before long, two percent of the population owned 50 percent of the land and tenant farmers paid up to 70 percent of their harvest to the landlord. The French maintained monopolies on the production of alcohol, opium, and salt. They imported rubber trees for a new industry that was controlled by a handful of non-natives.

The French abolished the old mandarin system of government and substituted their own administration and administrators. Vietnamese could only gain access to the very lowest civil service positions, and only then if they were French-speaking Roman Catholics. The natives who made it into the civil administration were poorly paid and limited in prospects. Even the lowliest Frenchman in service earned at least six times what the highest paid Vietnamese made. Moreover, Vietnam became a dumping ground for Frenchmen who aspired to civil careers but for whom there was no work at home. The French used more administrators to govern 30 million Vietnamese than the British used to rule 325 million Indians.[12] This enormous administrative superstructure had to be paid for somehow, and most of it came from punitive taxation of the Vietnamese.

Nationalists who rebelled against the French, and there were many, were harshly punished with harsh prison terms or death. Portable guillotines were sent around the countryside to deal with offenders. The Hao Lo prison, which gained notoriety during America's war with Vietnam as the "Hanoi Hilton," was constructed by the French to cage unruly Vietnamese.[13]

In 1890, a future revolutionary was born into the Nguyen family of Nghe An Province. He was named Nguyen Sinh Cung and would be later known to the world by one of his nom-de-guerre, Ho Chi Minh. Ho's father came from a peasant family but against all odds had become an educated man. His education carried him to a position as a minor official in the puppet Imperial court that was controlled by the French, and there he was exposed to first-hand evidence of foreign domination. This experience fostered a violent anti-French bias that was passed along to his children. His daughter, who was caught smuggling weapons to Vietnamese rebels, was sentenced to prison for life. His eldest son became a patriot-writer who penned petition after petition to the French to protest the living conditions of his people and to demand independence.

Party history tells us that the youngest son, who was to become Ho Chi Minh, began his revolutionary career at age five, carrying messages between groups of anti-French rebels. A bright lad, Ho listened to tales of Vietnamese heroes and plots to achieve Vietnam's freedom. He became educated and for a time taught school. When he was twenty-two he shipped on a French liner and landed in New York and later Paris, where he found himself in the middle of a large Vietnamese expatriate community, a revolutionary breeding ground. A thin, almost frail, man Ho was charismatic and intellectual. He became immersed in the virtues of socialism and then in the teachings of Lenin. Sympathetic biographers also credit him with personifying the six Confucian virtues of wisdom, benevolence, sincerity, righteousness, moderation, and harmony. He attracted an intensely loyal following in no time and remained abroad for thirty years. In his absence, insurrection at home continued apace.[14]

In 1930 a major event catalyzed the Vietnamese. On the night of February 8-9 a group of rebels attacked a French fort. The French responded with widespread air and ground attacks that probably killed more innocent civilians, including a good number of women and children, than revolutionaries. The resulting outrage fueled general fighting, which spread throughout the country and consumed lives and property for most of the year.[15] To dampen the violence, the French began a grim purge of anti-French revolutionaries. Ho Chi Minh was tried *in absentia* and sentenced to death. Others were caught and executed, and still more were sentenced to long prison terms from which few emerged. Vo Nguyen Giap, who was to become Vietnam greatest military commander in the wars against the French and the

Americans, barely escaped his pursuers and went into exile in China. His wife and infant daughter were captured and both died in prison, his wife after being subjected to barbarous tortures.[16]

Ho left Europe and arrived in China near the Vietnamese border in 1941. There he met Giap for the first time, and the two men formed a bond that would last until Ho's death in 1969.[17] Their arrival coincided with a new occupier of Vietnam, the Japanese. Ho and Giap collaborated with the American OSS against the Japanese and dreamed of post-war Vietnamese independence.[18] Just two weeks after Japan's defeat in 1945, Ho stepped up to a podium in Hanoi and gave a speech that was loosely based on an inflammatory document from another time—the American Declaration of Independence. He affirmed Vietnam to be a free and independent nation that would now govern itself without outside intervention.[19] The French were having none of it and moved immediately to crush Ho's movement.

Ho and Giap had begun building military units from the self-defense forces that had been formed among non-ethnic Vietnamese mountain tribes during the early forties at the time of the Japanese occupation. The first platoon, the genesis of what was to become a powerful army, was organized in 1944. It was called the Tuyen Truyen Giai Phong Quan, or Armed Propaganda and Liberation Unit. The emphasis on propaganda was no mistake; it reflected the Vietnamese experience against foreigners. Ho's idea was to remind his soldiers that all power came from the people.[20] Giap, like his long-ago predecessor Dao, understood the need to be one with the nation's inhabitants. Although a publicly stated goal of the United States in Vietnam was to win the hearts and minds of the people, the French and later most Americans believed technology and superior firepower to be sufficient to achieve their aims. An oft-repeated phrase during America's war in Vietnam was, "Grab 'em by the balls, and their hearts and minds will follow."[21]

Giap sent his forces headlong against the French shortly after Ho's independence speech. The results were disastrous. In the beginning the insurgents took countless casualties as they attempted to employ conventional tactics against superior technology. It quickly became evident to Giap and his officers that, in order to overcome French superiority in numbers of men, firepower, aircraft, and mobility, the Vietnamese would have to fall back on the tactics of their forebears. Using such tactics Giap was not to win many battles against the French. He did not have to, he needed only enough to make them quit. He took a page from the book of Tran Hung Dao, leader of the Vietnamese against the Mongols, who had said, "The enemy must fight his battles far from his home base for a long time. . . . We must further weaken him by drawing him into protracted campaigns. Once his initial dash is broken, it will be easier to destroy him."[22] Many years later it was American technology and firepower that bogged down against this philosophy. Anyone who fought in or studied America's war in Vietnam would recognize Giap's battle tactics against the French.

Giap learned never to seek a fight unless it was sure to be profitable, that he would win. The Americans, who were absolutely convinced of the superiority of their firepower, complained about this. They griped as if Giap's tactics made the enemy inferior, lesser men, ones who did not fight fair.

Moreover, Western firepower was a double-edged sword. It was difficult to control and often affected the innocent. Many Vietnamese who had no use for the communists were driven into their arms because of casualties within their families, dislocations, ruined businesses, and other forms of destruction caused by mass fire. Giap's propagandists were quick to exploit these mishaps to their own advantage.

Giap balanced his force ratio by such tactics as throwing a few rounds of gunfire at smaller outposts, just enough to wear down the inhabitants psychologically and to make the enemy use large amounts of supplies and men to guard them.

A lone guerrilla or a small team would mine roads and bridges at leisure, in the cool of the night. Then whole teams of French or American engineers and their security forces were forced to work in steam-bath heat to slowly, carefully, and stressfully sweep a road each time it had to be used.

Giap tried to make the French and the Americans afraid of *everything*. No unit was without at least one tale of the child who rolled a grenade into their midst, of the old woman who acted as a forward observer for enemy mortars, of the ARVN sergeant or officer who turned out to be a member of the Viet Cong. The list seemed endless. And then there were the ubiquitous booby traps, which, in some areas, caused up to 80 percent of French or American casualties. The French called this process *grignotage*, the slow nibbling away of their morale by all possible means.

Giap also insisted that each unit in the field be responsible for itself. If it got into trouble, it had to get itself out; even if it was faced with complete destruction, it could expect no help. The opposite side of this coin worked very much to the communists' advantage. They would ambush or attack a unit and be ready, as well, to ambush the relief force that the French or Americans invariably sent. Sometimes they would suck in several units in sequence, inflict terrible damage on them, and then withdraw when they, themselves, were threatened. The French, and particularly the Americans, risked large numbers of men and significant resources in attempts to save a small unit or even just one man.

Visions of the Alamo or Custer's Last Stand will not permit the American military psyche to do anything else.

CHAPTER 2

AMERICA TOUCHES THE TAR BABY

Before the Gulf of Tonkin incident in August 1964, the United States might have withdrawn from Vietnam without much furor. Politicians are rarely short of excuses, and if their imaginations let them down there were a couple of handy rationales lying about that were hardly used. President Dwight Eisenhower's dictum against getting involved in an Asian land war was one. The instability of the rotating governments of South Vietnam was another.

It was unlikely that a "Who lost Vietnam?" question would raise the hue and cry of the "Who lost China?" crowd a decade earlier, but the fact was that 1964 was a presidential election year. Although incumbent President Lyndon Johnson painted Republican nominee Senator Barry Goldwater as a war candidate, Johnson could not appear to be weak. He was a Texan, dammit, with all the pop-mythology baggage that the label carried. He regarded himself as a macho-man. Some months after Johnson's election, at a small White House meeting, Supreme Court Justice Arthur Goldberg asked the President why we were in Vietnam. Johnson unzipped his fly, pulled out his penis, and said, "This is why."[1] All of this became a moot point after the North Vietnamese appeared to throw down the gauntlet with patrol-boat attacks against U.S. Navy warships in August 1964. Never mind that the

United States had supported armed incursions against North Vietnam for a decade and that its Operation DeSoto naval patrols may have violated North Vietnam's territorial waters.[2]

The North Vietnamese attacks were seized upon as the perfect excuse to demonstrate just a tiny bit of that good old American military might, to show those North Vietnamese boys who they were dealing with. President Johnson authorized retaliatory strikes against Vietnamese military targets by American carrier-based aircraft. Over the next few months a series of escalating incidents, within and without South Vietnam, raised the profile of Vietnam, to say nothing of the testosterone levels, within President Lyndon Johnson's administration and brought Vietnam to the margins of American public perception. But the escalating incidents were not the most important legacy of this period. The corner was turned when Lyndon Johnson asked for, and Congress naively gave him, a blank check to conduct an undeclared war in Southeast Asia.[3]

Not everyone within the administration was sanguine about America's prospects in Vietnam. As early as 1963, John McCone, director of the Central Intelligence Agency (CIA), expressed doubts to President Kennedy about the efficacy of American efforts. His view of the adventure in Vietnam was that it was based on "complete lack of intelligence" and "exceedingly dangerous . . . " His views were dismissed as "out of step with policy."[4]

In April 1964 the U.S. Joint Chiefs authorized a war game, Sigma-I-64, to study the effects of heightened bombing of North Vietnam. Conducted by teams of military officers ranked lieutenant colonel through brigadier general and their civilian counterparts from the intelligence agencies, the results of the game were not encouraging. The conclusion was that the American position would go from bad to worse and would result in two unattractive choices—either a great expansion of the war against the North or an American de-escalation.[5] The hawks in the administration did not believe the findings, so five months later a second exercise, Sigma-II-64, was conducted. This time the rank and policy-making level of the participants was considerably higher, and the group included some of the more militant military and civilian players. Among them were Chairman of the Joint Chiefs of Staff General Earle Wheeler, air power advocate General Curtis LeMay, Deputy Secretary of Defense Cyrus Vance, and National Security Advisor McGeorge Bundy. Nevertheless, the results of SIGMA II were no more promising than the earlier version. Shocked by the results, Robert J. Meyer, a CIA participant, wrote a damning criticism of the American effort in Vietnam, questioning not only the effect of air power against the north but also the ability of large numbers of American ground troops to defeat an insurgent enemy with a credible political message.[6] The policy makers thought that they knew better and Meyer's warnings went unheeded.

In the subsequent months, conditions in South Vietnam quickly deteriorated under communist pressure. By the end of 1964 the Viet Cong were operating in regimental strength in several places with little serious challenge from the Saigon government.[7] Giap had three full divisions within fifty miles of Saigon, which he hoped to isolate when the time was right. In February 1965 U.S. Army LtGen Bruce Palmer visited all of the four military regions into which South Vietnam was divided. He found that the Viet Cong controlled or had cut railroads, highways, and other lines of communication in major expanses of the country, and threatened normal social and economic life. South Vietnam was poised on the brink of collapse.

General Westmoreland's deputy, Gen John Throckmorton, visited Danang, the major population center in the I Corps Military Region (I Corps), the northernmost region of South Vietnam, and pronounced it in grave danger.[8] Not only was it threatened from the ground, there were fears that the North Vietnamese would use their Soviet-supplied aircraft to stage a strike against the critical Danang base. This base had become increasingly important to the Johnson administration because the President had decided to proceed with Operation Rolling Thunder, a series of bombing attacks against North Vietnam. Danang was to be an important launching site for some of these aircraft.

In order to protect the base against possible air attack from North Vietnam, Westmoreland requested a Hawk antiaircraft missile unit and was given the U.S. Marine Corps' 1st Light Antiaircraft Missile (LAAM) Battalion. Two Marine infantry battalions, the 3d Battalion, 9th Marines (3/9), and the 1st Battalion, 3d Marines (1/3), landed on March 8 to back up the missile unit and defend the field from ground attack. Marine infantry battalions were deployed to defend the Danang field because their missile unit was already there, and Westmoreland decided that this would preclude inter-service confusion. The Marines' mission was to occupy and defend critical terrain features and certain facilities to secure the airfield. In no uncertain terms, they were instructed to "not, repeat not," engage in day-to-day actions against the VC.[9] Lyndon Johnson was worried about public reaction to sending in

Marines as opposed to men from another service. He told Robert McNamara, "the psychological impact of the Marines are coming is going to be a *bad* one. And I know enough to know that. And I know that every mother is going to say, '*Uh-oh this is it!*'. . . . Damned if I don't know why we can't find some sort of a policeman beside the *Marines,* because a Marine is a guy that's got a *dagger* in his hand. And that's going to put the *flag* up. An Army boy is not so much, and a Navy boy is not so much. But . . . "[10]

Lyndon Johnson had his own doubts about the ability of America to win in Vietnam, but they were never publicly stated. He told McNamara on February 26, 1965, "I don't think anything is going to be as bad as losing, but I don't see any way of winning."[11]

On March 24, just after the first Marines landed in Vietnam, Assistant Aecretary of State for National Security Affairs John McNaughton outlined in a memo to his boss, Robert McNamara, the goals of the American activities in SVN (South Vietnam):

70%— to avoid a humiliating defeat (to our reputation as guarantor)

20%—to keep SVN (and the adjacent) territory from Chinese hands.

10%—to permit people of SVN to enjoy a better way of life. Also—to emerge from crisis without unacceptable taint from methods used.

Not—to "help a friend," although it would be hard to stay in if asked out.[12]

As McNaughton's memorandum makes clear, in March 1965 the main consideration in America's expansion of the war in Vietnam was *not* to make the world safe for democracy, *not* to keep all of Southeast Asia from falling to the Communists, and certainly *not* to "help a friend." The United States was getting further in because it would be too *embarrassing to America's interests* to get out. By this date 581 Americans had died in Vietnam. This was less than 1 percent of the eventual total.

The landing of the Marines at this point was regarded by the Johnson administration as a one-time affair to fulfill a specific requirement. With his election in the bag and the blank check from Congress in his pocket, the American President could afford to be slightly more aggressive in Vietnam. Nevertheless, his true love was his Great Society program, a series of domestic achievements that would be the capstone of his political career. Vietnam was an irritant, a distraction. Johnson expected that more American pressure would, "nail that coonskin to the wall," thus freeing him to concentrate on domestic issues.

As they were to do throughout the war, the Americans gravely underestimated the price the communists were willing to pay. The North Vietnamese met escalation with escalation. Most important was their decision to meet increased American presence through the infiltration of regular North Vietnamese Army (NVA) troops to the south. Up until the beginnings of the conventional American troop buildup, the Vietnamese communists called their conflict with the southern half of the country and its American arms and advisors a "special war." Once faced with the challenge of standard American military units, the communist policy evolved quickly into "direct war." True, the communists would continue to wage an unconventional war to offset the American's superior firepower and mobility, but they expected to directly challenge American professional fighting units.[13]

Limiting the American buildup to just two Marine battalions was not to be. Army Chief of Staff Harold K. Johnson, who was in Vietnam during the Marine landings, returned to Washington with the recommendation for deployment of a U.S. Army division. Not yet ready to pay the political price for such a large increase, President Johnson authorized two additional Marine battalions in National Security Memorandum 328, issued on April 6, 1965.[14] This document also directed a crucial "change of mission for all Marine battalions deployed in Vietnam to permit their more active use."

The trickle of battalions into the country was about to become a flood. Along with the deployment of additional Marine units came the deployment of bigger headquarters organizations. The headquarters element of the 3d Marine Division, commanded by MajGen William Collins came ashore to oversee Marine operations. A few weeks after his arrival General Collins left for the United States at the end of his normal tour. His replacement was Lewis W. Walt, who had just been promoted to major general a few days before his assignment and was thus the junior officer of that rank in the Marine Corps.

Lew Walt was a large, barrel-chested man (he wore a size 48-long coat), born in Kansas and raised in Colorado. He had been a football star at Colorado State University and was a war hero from World War II and Korea. He had won the Silver Star Medal at Guadalcanal for recovering wounded Marines under Japanese machine-gun fire. At Cape Gloucester, New Britain, in January 1944, he observed all six members of a Marine 37mm gun crew being killed or wounded as they tried to get their weapon to the top of a hill. Walt unhesitatingly rushed forward alone and began pushing the gun up the hill. Inspired by his action, several other Marines joined him. Upon reaching the crest of the hill Walt and his small group of men held off five furious Japanese counterattacks. He was awarded his first Navy Cross Medal for this effort. His second Navy Cross Medal came eight months later, on Peleliu. When both the commanding officer and the executive officer of a Marine infantry battalion were killed in a violent engagement with the enemy, Lew Walt rushed in and took command, reorganized the battalion, and led it on to its objective under intense fire.

Shortly after his assignment to Vietnam, Walt was promoted to lieutenant general; he would be the architect of Marine operations there for two years. General Walt's promotion came in the wake of moving the 1st Marine Aircraft Wing (1st MAW) to Vietnam. The combination infantry division and aircraft wing were designated the III Marine Expeditionary Force. A few days later this was changed to III Marine Amphibious Force (III MAF). The change was made because the "expeditionary" title was too reminiscent of the French Expeditionary Force, which had left Vietnam under a shadow. General Walt was the first commander of III MAF.

*   *   *

The makeshift quality of the Johnson administration's policies on Vietnam was already showing through. Within a few weeks, the United States shifted from a policy to protect an airfield to an "enclave strategy" whose most visible proponent was retired U.S. Army Gen James Gavin.[15] "Enclave strategy" meant that American forces would deploy in enclaves around major bases from which they would be permitted to conduct offensive operations within a fifty-mile radius. The enclave strategy was favored by many in the Marine Corps as being one of the first steps leading to pacification and population control. General Walt stated upon taking command in Vietnam, "With 100,000 people within 81mm mortar range of Danang, I had to be in the pacification business." Unfortunately for the conduct of the war, this approach also had a short life.

CHAPTER 3

THE FIELD CALLED "LITTLE MAN"[1]

The Marine Corps is an air-ground team so, along with the deployment of its infantry battalions into Vietnam, the call came for aircraft to follow. Marine helicopter squadrons had rotated in and out of the country in support of the ARVN and the Vietnamese Marines since 1962. Lieutenant Colonel Archie Clapp's Marine Medium Helicopter Squadron 362 (HMM-362) landed at Soc Trang on April 15, 1962, and operated out of a former Japanese airfield in the Mekong Delta. A succession of squadrons provided the Marines with invaluable information about operating in Vietnam. The operational designation of this effort was "Shufly." By early 1965 the helicopter commitment had grown to two squadrons. Now that the Marines had their own infantry in Vietnam, fixed-wing attack and fighter aircraft were added for close air support.

It became obvious that a second airfield for fixed-wing aircraft would be needed. The field in Danang was overcrowded with both Marine and Air Force squadrons, South Vietnamese aviation units, and logistics traffic. It had a single 10,000-foot runway that just a few years earlier had served as a provincial airport for that part of the country. Now it was tasked with being a major air base in a war zone.

In the words of a Marine aviator, Maj Al Bloom, Danang was "dangerous as hell." Several spectacular and tragically fatal accidents occurred there. Then there was "One-Shot Charlie," a Viet Cong who lived near the end of the runway and who cranked off a round at every aircraft that passed over his end of the field. The Americans never found him.

Thanks to the foresight of Marine LtGen Victor Krulak, the commander of Fleet Marine Force, Pacific (FMFPac), a site was already under study for the installation of a Short Airfield for Tactical Support (SATS).[2] It was about fifty miles south of Danang on a sandy coastal plain near the South China Sea. After reviewing the contingency plans for a rapid American buildup in South Vietnam, Krulak recommended this particular location to his boss, Commander-in-Chief, U.S. Pacific Fleet (CinCPac), Adm U. S. Grant Sharp. Admiral Sharp agreed and fired it up the line to Washington. On March 12, 1965, Secretary of Defense Robert McNamara approved the installation. General Krulak decided the new base was to be called Chulai.

"Chulai" is not a Vietnamese name. When Krulak was a young officer in China in the years prior to World War II, he learned the Chinese characters that approximated the Chinese pronunciation of his name. The Vietnamese pronounced these same characters "Chulai." They mean "little man" which, given Krulak's 5 feet, 5 inch height, seemed appropriate.[3] Despite his small size, Krulak was a famous Marine, and a hero. His classmates at the Naval Academy had dubbed him "Brute" because of his diminutive stature. A story was that to make sure he made the minimum height requirement for Annapolis he had had someone whack him on the head with a board to raise a knot the day of his entrance physical. Brute Krulak went on to win the Navy Cross Medal in World War II, become the youngest major general in the Marine Corps, and served as special advisor for counter-insurgency warfare to Presidents Kennedy and Johnson. He possessed a quick mind and boundless energy.

The Marines, looking back at their extensive experience in fighting in primitive countries, had long thought about the advantages of being able to quickly construct and operate from 2,000-foot-long airfields that could handle two or three aircraft squadrons. As originally envisioned, these bases would be constructed on the site of undeveloped or abandoned airfields.

As naval aviators, Marine pilots are qualified to operate from the confines of an aircraft carrier deck. The problem now was to move the operation ashore. In addition to an airstrip there would have to be taxiways; hardstand; fueling, maintenance and rearmament facilities; and air traffic control. Moreover, since they would be operating from very short fields, they needed something like the catapults used on ships to launch aircraft, and arresting gear to recover them. The Marine Corps Development Center at Quantico, Virginia, pushed for an entire expeditionary airfield that could be assembled and operational in seventy-two to ninety-six hours. Various projects were underway to fulfill these requirements.

In 1960 the Marines conducted a major exercise to test their theories at Ping Tung, Taiwan. There they constructed and operated from a SATS airfield in an expeditionary environment. While the operation was deemed a success, there were many kinks to be ironed out, and the Taiwan exercise was, after all, conducted in a peaceful environment.

One of the essential needs at Chulai was for runway and taxiway material that would withstand impact and static loads of aircraft, and jet exhaust temperature. After much experimentation, the AM-2 aluminum plank was selected. Two by twelve feet in size and 140 pounds in weight, each plank was capable of being interlocked in place.

The arresting gear for carrier use was modified. It was a dry friction, energy-absorbing device with a wire pendant that stretched across the runway. Marine fixed-wing aircraft, like those of their Navy brethren, were equipped with tailhooks that the pilot dropped when landing in order to snag the arresting gear. The aircraft recovery gear developed for Chulai worked, and it later became standard in the Marine Corps.

A problem with launching still needed to be overcome. A land-based catapult was under development but was not available in March 1965,when the decision was made to build the airfield at Chulai. The Marines decided to temporarily overcome the problem with the use of jet assisted take-off (JATO) bottles. These were essentially rockets, temporarily attached to the aircraft for launch and then jettisoned upon takeoff. The Marines modified their small A4 Skyhawk attack aircraft to use them.

The amphibious bulk fuel system, developed for vehicular traffic, was modified with the proper fuel-dispensing devices to service aircraft.

A problem the Quantico planners did not envision was the terrain on which this airstrip would be built. There was no abandoned airfield there, or even soil. The entire area was covered with soft sand. But

Chulai was by the sea, near a body of water, tucked in behind a peninsula that could be developed into an LST (Landing Ship, Tank) port. A port that could handle up to six LSTs was quickly developed, and it supported nearly all the considerable logistics requirements for the field and the aircraft. Direct supply or reinforcement from the sea was a major advantage. The site could also be defended without too much difficulty, and there was a relatively small Vietnamese population to be relocated.

On May 7, 1965, the 2d Battalion, 4th Marines (2/4), came ashore to secure and guard the site. Colonel James McClanahan's 4th Marines command post landed to coordinate the operation and Cdr J. M. Bannister's 10th Seabees (Naval Mobile Construction Battalion 10) followed the Marines onto the beach to build the first SATS under combat conditions.

*   *   *

The 2d Battalion, 4th Marines, was part of the 1st Marine Brigade, based in Hawaii, and came to Vietnam, along with its parent unit after briefly pausing at Okinawa. Lieutenant Colonel Joseph R. "Bull" Fisher commanded the battalion, and most of his Marines had been together for more than two years. They trained hard and well, and understood each other's strengths and weaknesses. In many cases they knew each other's families.

Like all Marines units, 2/4 was a force in readiness and could be called at any time to deploy to a combat area. But the guns of the Korean War had been silent for twelve years and most of the men expected to serve their tours with 2/4 in peace until rotation home or expiration of active service caught up with them. In the spring of 1965, however, signs began to accumulate that conditions were changing. Their anticipated participation in Operation Silver Lance in California was cancelled. The Marines were asked to make out wills, take care of pay allotments for their families, and stow personal effects. They were subjected to on-again, off-again, hurry-up-and-wait drills, until one day they packed up and boarded ship. Ostensibly they were sailing for Okinawa. In their guts, the Marines knew better. Vietnam became, very intently, the object of their thoughts and discussions. They did spend a few weeks on Okinawa, where they test-fired weapons, got their vaccinations up to date, and stored the last of their civilian clothes. They formed around-the-clock work parties to load ships with ammunition—live ammunition this time, not the blanks they were accustomed to using. They also trained hard and kept themselves in good physical condition to meet the rigors of combat, should they be called. Some of the officers and staff non-commissioned officers (SNCOs) went to Vietnam on temporary assignments and came back with daunting tales about the heat, the enemy, and the people. The Marines enjoyed some good liberty on Okinawa, but Lieutenant Colonel Fisher had daily 0500 formations where the hard-party guys could often be seen heaving up their last meals into the bushes at the fringes of the early morning physical workouts.

THE LANDINGS

Fisher's battalion finally got top secret orders for going into Vietnam and once more boarded ship. Its mission was to protect the newly designated airfield location at Chulai. The Marines were briefed on their destination and assignment en route. On the night before landing, nerves were on edge and everyone was restless. Bull Fisher, a Marine's Marine who had seen many campaigns, knew what to do. He ordered his officers and SNCOs to circulate among the men throughout the night and make sure everyone was okay. As dawn broke, the Marines gathered on deck, formed into their boat teams, and went down the nets. The landing craft circled until all were in the water and loaded, and then they lined up by pre-arranged plan and headed for the beach. When the ramps dropped, 2/4 rushed ashore with weapons locked and loaded, ready to fight. The enemy declined the invitation, however, and the landing was peaceful.

The Marines quickly moved inland and went all the way to secure National Route 1, the two-lane highway that runs the entire length of Vietnam, from north to south. Having secured that objective, they were wondering what to do next when they heard the roar of vehicles descending on them down the highway from the north. They immediately shifted weapons in that direction, uncertain of what and who was coming to greet them. Suddenly, American-made 2 - ton trucks came into view and stopped outside of their lines. The South Vietnamese drivers dropped the tailgates and helped dozens of pretty young Vietnamese women to the ground. The women hurried over to the Marines and draped garlands of flowers around their necks to welcome them to Vietnam. Despite the heat and sand, the Marines thought they were off to a good start in Vietnam.

The 2/4 command post (CP) was established on Hill 43, near the northwest corner of the airfield, and there the battalion staff planned airfield security. The Marines wasted no time establishing outposts, and they began patrolling that very day.

A week later, on May 12, the 3d Battalion, 3d Marines, (3/3), came ashore to bolster the defense force. Commanded by LtCol Colonel William D. Hall, 3/3 had transplaced to Okinawa the previous January. (Transplacement was a pre-Vietnam War system of replacing infantry battalions and aircraft squadrons a unit at a time. A new unit would form and train in the United States for some months and then depart for the Far East to replace another unit, which, having finished its thirteen-month tour, would rotate back to the U.S.) Hall's 3/3 was one of the last units to transplace to Asia under the old system. Like the Marines of 2/4, most of these men had been in the unit for two years or longer, and they worked hard and well together. 2/4 relinquished the southern airstrip security sector to 3/3, which also began a series of defensive activities.

The landing force commander at Chulai was BriGen Marion E. Carl, one of the Corps' top aviators—the Marine Corps' first air ace, a hero of the Battle of Midway and the Guadalcanal Campaign, and a two-time recipient of the Navy Cross Medal. General Carl had shot down eighteen Japanese aircraft in World War II.

General Carl began loading his 1st Marine Brigade in Hawaii on March 10, 1965, for transport to the Western Pacific. Fortuitously, shipping had arrived to carry the brigade to California to participate in Operation Silver Lance in February. When the brigade's orders were changed, the ships were on hand to haul the Marines west rather than east. General Krulak had not marked off exactly where the Chulai airfield should go, so his seasoned aviator, General Carl, determined its precise location.

The combination of sand, salt air, and heat greatly hampered everything the Marines and Seabees did. Unloading the ships and moving materials across the terrain was a formidable task. Equipment broke down at rates far higher than normal, and the American troops were worn down as well. Tracked vehicles had to be used to move rubber-tired ones.

Private First Class Glen Johnson, an engineer, had learned to drive a jeep in sand on Operation Steel Pike in Spain the year before. His successful but scary technique was to put the jeep in low-range, four-wheel drive, shift to second gear, and put his foot all the way to the floor. And they *went.* They were able to fly across the tops of sand dunes in the days prior to the Seabees getting roads in.

Not far inland from the beach the sand gave way to a red soil called laterite. The plan was to use that on the airstrip, as a sub-base between the aluminum matting and the sand. But before that could be done it was necessary to build a road from where the laterite was located to where it was to be placed. Under these conditions no one expected the airfield to be finished in three or four days. The irrepressible General Krulak bet Army MajGen Richard G. Stilwell, the MACV chief of staff, a case of Scotch that a squadron would be operating there within thirty days.

LIFE IN THE SANDBOX

The Marines found plenty to do while the Seabees were building the field. Their first task was to get acclimated. The sand was too hot to walk on in bare feet during the day, and it did not permit the preparation of fighting holes the way soil did. And it got into *everything.* Weapons, radios, vehicles, tools, drinking water, clothing, food, everything the Marines had seemed to be covered with a layer of sand. At least there was plenty of it for sandbags, so the Marines constructed above-ground bunkers with sandbag walls. For the roofs, as protection against mortar attack, they "liberated" pieces of the runway matting from the Seabees and piled sandbags on them. Living under these conditions was difficult but not so bad for seasoned young Marines with a lot of experience living in the field. They ate C-rations out of cans, bathed in the South China Sea, slept on the ground, patrolled and stood watches, and stood watches and patrolled. The Marines of this era were still armed with the M14 rifle which had just replaced the venerable M1 in 1962.

Both battalions established outposts that were constantly manned on prominent terrain features around the base. 2/4 named theirs after fish, the Catfishes and the Perches. 3/3 called theirs other things. One was called Hickory, because the sergeant initially in charge was from Kentucky. These small strongholds, rarely manned by more than a squad, soon became the objects of probes and sniper rounds from the enemy.

Inevitably, combat casualties occurred. Some Marines were hit while on patrol, some were the victims of booby traps, and a few were casualties of their own stupidity. One afternoon two senior staff NCOs from the air group passed outbound through one of 3/3's outposts. The Marine in charge of the checkpoint was junior in rank to these two men, and they refused to heed his warning not to go into a neighboring village. They disappeared down a road and were never seen again. The Marines heard later that the Viet Cong captured them, marched them about a mile from the base, and shot and buried them. Their bodies were never found.[4]

Relations with the villagers were characterized by caution on both sides. The enemy told the Vietnamese bad things about the Americans, and the elders remembered bad things about the French. As the Marines spent more time in the area, the mutual mistrust and suspicion declined. The Marines, with decades of experience in the pacification business in Latin America, put a lot of thought and effort into their programs. They sent medical doctors and corpsmen to the villages to hold sick call. These men treated minor ailments and inoculated hundreds of Vietnamese, many for the first time in their lives, against such diseases as typhus, cholera, and yellow fever. The Marines built and furnished schools and medical clinics, they repaired churches, they helped built windmills to pump water, and they assisted with other agricultural projects. Some of the money and material for these projects came directly from the U.S. government, but much of it came from churches and civic organizations in the United States. Not all projects were successful. A schoolhouse built by Sgt Pat Finton and other engineers was burned to the ground one night. The enemy bribed a small boy to do the deed.

The war forced decisions on young men of a kind they never thought they would have to make. One night a Marine unit led by GySgt Gene Breeze set up an ambush along the beach to intercept VC who might try to infiltrate from that direction. When dawn broke the Marines spotted three armed and uniformed enemy headed right for them. As the VC approached to within fifty meters, an old man and young girl suddenly appeared and headed across the beach at an angle between the VC and the concealed Marines. The VC spotted the Marines, grabbed the civilians, and forced them to march ahead of them right toward the American position. The pre-arranged signal to trip the ambush was for Gunny Breeze to fire his shotgun. He hesitated a moment because of the civilians but realized a fire fight was unavoidable no matter what he did. Aiming carefully over the young girl's head, at one of the VC, he pulled the trigger. His weapon misfired and he had to shout at one of the other Marines to set off the ambush. When the dust had settled there were no VC bodies to be found, just blood. The little girl was hurt, creased in the forehead by a bullet and wounded seriously in the leg. She was immediately evacuated to a hospital, where she fully recovered.

An M79 grenade launcher was stolen in the 3/3 sector. For the next few days the Marines searched for it by patrolling the neighboring villages in the company of the village chiefs and, in some cases, troops from the Popular Forces troops, a Vietnamese militia. They discovered that the young lad who had stolen the M79 had sold it to the enemy. To the horror of the Marines the village chief immediately pulled out his pistol and executed the boy on the spot.

At the An Tan Bridge, in the 2/4 sector, Marines killed two VC who tried to infiltrate at night. They removed a map from one of the bodies and found that it was complete to the point of having on it some changes in the defensive positions made that very same day. It turned out that the son of a nearby village chief was a spy for the enemy and had drawn the map.

It was apparent that the Vietnamese people were sharply divided, but it was impossible to tell which side most were on. Those who favored the Americans were incredibly cruel to those who helped the communists, and vice versa. Some played each side against the other. It was a confusing and demoralizing situation. The war was fragmented.

Decisions that in other conflicts would have been made at much higher levels were dropped into the hands of the small-unit leaders, the junior officers, sergeants, and corporals. There were no front lines, and there was no rear. One Marine recalled that the men he admired most were those he called the "old-salt corporals." These young men, many of whom were still in their teens, could lead squad-size patrols several hundreds, if not thousands of meters from main positions. They could read maps, use compasses, call in artillery and air, evacuate their wounded and dead, communicate, and fight.

Rules of engagement sorely hampered the Marines in the early days. They began by not even being allowed to have a magazine in their weapons. They could not initiate a fight, only return fire at someone who fired at them first. When the rules were relaxed a bit, they were permitted to shoot at someone who was clearly an enemy soldier. This was very difficult in a situation in which the enemy was not uniformed and was often a farmer by day and a guerrilla by night.

The Marines' own perimeter constituted their tactical area of responsibility (TAOR), and they were not to fire outside of their own lines without permission from the South Vietnamese. Permission to fire small arms or use supporting arms was difficult to obtain. While Marines waited for the Vietnamese chain of command to give approval the enemy often slipped away.

The era of jungle boots and jungle uniforms lay in the future. All-leather boots, designed for other climates, rotted here. Likewise, the uniforms were entirely too heavy and too hot for Vietnam. Water was a constant problem. The usual two canteens per man were not enough, and since the water was often very, very warm and frequently treated with chemical tablets to sanitize it, it was unpleasant to drink. Small-unit leaders constantly had to force the men to hydrate themselves despite the poor quality of the water. Heat casualties were common in the beginning, but as the Marines became acclimated and familiar with their environment this became less of a problem.

The Marines had to learn to use helicopters in this sandy, hot, humid setting. Although they had practiced their helicopter doctrine for years, this was the first big test. Newsman Harry Reasoner later said this about helicopters: "The thing is, helicopters are different than planes. An airplane by its nature wants to fly and if it is not interfered with too strongly by unusual events or by a deliberately incompetent pilot, it will fly. A helicopter does not want to fly. It is maintained in the air by a variety of forces and controls, working in opposition to each other; and if there is any disturbance in the delicate balance, the helicopter stops flying immediately and disastrously. There is no such thing as a gliding helicopter. This is why being a helicopter pilot is so different from being an airplane pilot; and why, in generality, airplane pilots are open, clear eyed, extroverts and helicopter pilots are brooders, introspective anticipators of trouble. They know that if anything bad has not happened, it is about to."[5]

The helicopter these Marines flew was the H-34. It was 67 feet, 7 inches long from the front of the main rotor disc to the end of the tail rotor, and it stood 14 feet, 3 inches tall. The crew was four in number—pilot, co-pilot, crew chief, and gunner. The bird weighed about 10,000 pounds and mounted two M60 machine guns, one in the cargo hatch on the starboard side and the other in a smaller window on the port side. The crew chief and gunner operated these weapons.

Depending on heat and humidity the H-34 could carry about seven combat-loaded Marines or about ten Vietnamese. The dirt, salt, and sand of the operating areas played hell with the maintenance schedules for the H-34s. Engines that had been programmed for a thousand operational hours were now failing at six hundred hours or less. At least one gave up its mechanical ghost at about three hundred and sixty hours. Tail-rotor and main-rotor blades failed at an alarming rate. In order to prolong their lives one squadron put ordnance tape over the leading rotor edges to reduce wear. Adding to the maintenance woes was the fact that the squadrons were flying twice the number of planned hours per week. The efforts of the ground crews to keep the birds in the air bordered on the heroic.

The problems with helicopters reflected a larger logistics issue the Marine Corps had. The Corps was a light-infantry force designed to be an expeditionary force that was to seize and hold beachheads long enough for heavier American or allied forces to get ashore and fight the long-haul battles. The Marines who went ashore in Vietnam found themselves used as a permanent ground force, and their units were to stay for the duration of the war. The Marine Corps was confronted with enormous and unprecedented difficulties in establishing and maintaining the necessary logistics base for its long-term operations.

Helicopter-borne maneuvers were to dominate American operational thinking throughout the entire war. A couple of days before Starlite a pilot from HMM-361, Capt Howard Henry, flew some Marines into an ARVN outpost. They took some fire from the ground; the crew chief, SSgt Coy Overstreet, thought that it sounded like the clatter of an old Browning Automatic Rifle. He looked for the enemy and spotted him among some bushes. While Captain Henry flew the helo in circles, Overstreet and the VC soldier got into an automatic weapons duel. The Marine finally drove the man out into the open without his weapon, headed for a bomb crater. "What the hell," Henry told his crew, "let's go capture him," and he put the bird down next to the crater. Another crewmember, Staff Sergeant Maynard, covered the man with his machine gun while Overstreet ran over, bodily picked the VC up, threw him over his shoulder, ran back to the chopper, and tossed him inside. The crew immediately delivered him to intelligence for questioning.

On another occasion Maj Al Bloom flew a night medevac to pick up casualties after a fire fight. The Marines on the ground had no flashlights, so Bloom had one of them light matches. He extinguished the aircraft lights and put his bird into a tight downward spiral in order to reduce the chances that the enemy on the ground would see the foot-long blue exhaust plume. Guided solely by the matches Bloom landed in a flooded paddy and loaded the casualties. As he did, mortar rounds landed all around him, but they did not detonate because of the water in the paddy. He finally lifted off with a prayer of thanks and was gaining altitude when the Marines on the ground called once more to say they had another casualty. As Bloom descended for a second time the mission was cancelled. The casualty had died.

*   *   *

Just a few days before Starlite, on August 12-13, twenty four Marine Air Group 16 (MAG-16) helicopters participated in the first night helicopter assault in Vietnam. (MAG-16 was the intermediate command for helicopters, the aviation equivalent of a regimental headquarters. Its CO reported to the 1st MAW commanding general, who in turn reported to General Walt.]

The aircraft landed with the aid of parachute flares, debarked the infantry and returned to Danang without incident. Fourteen birds from LtCol Lloyd Childers's HMM-361, six from HMM-261, and four from Marine Observation Squadron 2 (VMO-2) participated. They lifted 245 Marines into the operation area.

The helicopters were organized into two initial flights of ten each with the four VMO-2 UH-1 Huey gunships flying cover. The two waves took off at 2347 and 2350, respectively; upon landing their Marines the helicopters returned to Danang and picked up the third and fourth waves.

The operation was in the Ca De Song (Elephant) Valley, near Danang. It was not a night for the superstitious to be aloft. The landings took place at midnight on Friday the 13th under a full moon. Ninety-six crewman, including officers, flew the mission, which is believed to be the first night helicopter assault in history. They flew into Elephant Valley because of a report that fifty Viet Cong would be coming in there at night.

The infantrymen were from Hotel Company, 2/3, augmented by a platoon from Foxtrot Company. The landing zones were prepped with artillery, which was also supposed to muffle the sounds of the incoming choppers.

After the artillery, four Hueys went over the objective area as bait, to see if they could draw fire. No one reacted.

A minute from touchdown, as the choppers were rotoring through a 2,700-foot mountain pass, an Air Force plane dropped a pattern of parachute flares to illuminate the zone. Even with this illumination, some helicopter pilots had their crew chiefs lean out of doors and to make five-foot estimates as to the distance to the ground. The Marines were landed perfectly.

In terms of killing the enemy, the operation was not a success. It only netted one VC KIA. Thirty suspects were detained, and a VC rocket launcher and grenades were captured.

CHULAI OPERATIONS BEGIN

The strip and some taxiway were marginally ready by Memorial Day to receive fixed-wing aircraft, but the designated airplanes were grounded in the Philippines by bad weather. After a few days' delay, they finally arrived at Chulai. Shortly after 0800 on June 1, Col John Noble, the commander of MAG-12, landed the first of four A4 Skyhawks on the new field. Two more flights quickly followed.

The aviators got down to business without delay. On the same day they landed, a combat mission took off from the new airfield led by LtCol Robert W. Baker, the commanding officer of Marine Attack Squadron 225 (VMA-225).

VMA-225 had an unusual history and was, at this time, one of the best-trained attack squadrons in the Marine Corps. In addition to their normal qualifications the crews were trained for "special weapons" delivery, that is, they could deliver nuclear bombs. In order to reach this high level of expertise, the squadron personnel were stabilized far longer than normal and had worked together for more than two years. This long relationship meant that the unit functioned unusually well as a team and enjoyed very high morale. They won the Commandant of the Marine Corps' Efficiency Trophy in 1963.[6]

In the beginning the squadrons could only fly about one mission per airplane per day because of the extremely primitive conditions at Chulai. The nature of the subsoil caused the arresting gear to require frequent resetting. The sand and red dust played hell with the aircraft and all associated equipment. It was extremely difficult to get the guns to feed properly. It was not unusual to go out on a strafing mission, begin a run on a target, and have one gun not fire at all while the other gun fired one round before it jammed.[7]

Ordnance was difficult to obtain. Very often the bombs available were what the pilots called "one-look bombs," the old high-drag bombs that looked like leftovers from World War II. They had bulbous shapes and square fins.[8] The A4 was a considerably higher speed aircraft than the bombers of World War II, and it didn't carry such bombs well. The bomb racks weren't configured to hold them, so it was extremely difficult for the ordnance people to load them on the airplane. They had to beat the square fins flat with sledgehammers, which gave the bombs unpredictable ballistics. Very often the pilots did not know where the bombs were going to fall or if they would detonate when they hit the ground. The general load of ordnance the A4 should have carried could be a combination of a full load of 20mm ammunition for the two wing-mounted cannon and eighteen 250-pound low-drag bombs; or combinations of Bull Pup missiles; napalm; low-drag bombs; multiple rocket packs of eighteen 2.75-inch rockets each, which could be rippled off, salvoed, or fired singly; and 5-inch Zuni rockets that came in packs of four. The rockets were particularly hard to come by in the early days.[9]

Although air operations were underway, General Krulak paid off his bet with General Stilwell, because an entire squadron was not operating in the designated time, only half of one. Nonetheless, three A4 squadrons were operational at Chulai by the end of July.

The airfield construction at Chulai was endless. Laterite was not doing the job, so after 8,000 feet of runway was constructed the field was redone, one half at a time, until the right sub-base combination was found. Before it was over, a new method evolved. It included packing the sand down, fixing it with a light layer of asphalt, and then using a thin plastic membrane to keep the rain from settling into the soil.

A catapult was installed in April 1966, eliminating the need for the JATO bottles. The following year, also, a concrete strip was begun just to the west of the SATS strip, and eventually two Marine air groups operated from the base. But those are other stories. The Chulai airstrip is, as of 2003, the longest in the country. The Vietnamese are building a commercial harbor and an oil refinery nearby and hope to turn the Chulai area into a major economic zone.

CHAPTER 4

CONTINUING ESCALATION

As the Marines at Chulai learned to fight a new kind of war there were major developments from both sides in troop deployments to South Vietnam. By June 1965 intelligence detected the presence of elements of the 325th North Vietnamese Army (NVA) Division in the south as well as evidence that the 308th NVA Division was on the way. General Westmoreland asked for the speedy deployment of additional forces, and on June 22 he was told that an additional forty-four combat battalions would be sent as soon as possible. America had fully embraced the tar baby and wouldn't be able to pry herself loose until a decade had passed and 58,000 lives had been expended.

It was at this point that the war of attrition that characterized the conflict in Vietnam got underway. General Westmoreland ended the enclave strategy in favor of taking the fight to the enemy main-force units in the mountains and jungles. The first search-and-destroy operations were conducted by U.S. Army units near Saigon in June. Although much criticized, the war of attrition was one of Westmoreland's few remaining options, because he resisted basing his effort on the type of pacification favored by the Marines, and the Johnson administration ruled out invasion of North Vietnam or even the full-scale application of military might against it.

ON THE OTHER SIDE OF THE RIVER

The base at Chulai was on the border between Quang Tin and Quang Ngai provinces. The south end of the field was just a few kilometers from the Tra Bong River, a broad tidal body. The area to the south of the Tra Bong, in Quang Ngai Province, was a traditional Viet Cong stronghold, and it held a special place in the history of Vietnam. It was from this region that the Nguyen Dynasty began its long and difficult movement southward to bring the rest of the country under its hegemony. It was a province in which armed resistance against the French was legendary. From 1868, when French occupied the country, through peasant revolts against pro-French bureaucrats in the 1930s, and up until the post-World War II anti-French activity, which ejected them from the country, the Vietnamese here had fought long and hard against foreigners and their indigenous representatives. In 1948 Ho Chi Minh had declared the province one of Vietnam's few "free zones," that is, a region free from the influence of both the French and the "puppet" emperor Bao Dai.[1] Diem's government attempted to "pacify" this anti-government stronghold through the forced relocation of most of its inhabitants into "strategic hamlets." Compelling natives to leave the only villages they had ever known and in which they had worshipped their ancestors for hundreds of years was a disaster. This policy of the South Vietnam government played right into the hand of the VC cadres, which used it as an example of oppression by a puppet organization, the Republic of Vietnam government, of another Western invader, the United States. Despite the government's best efforts the area was strongly pro-Viet Cong and strongly anti-Saigon.

Inasmuch as this difficult region was closest to 3/3's TAOR that battalion began to patrol south of the river. At first the Marines sent platoons into the area. When platoons ran into trouble, the Marines sent over entire companies. But every time the Marines raised the stakes, the enemy did the same. The VC did not stand and fight; they used methods designed to distract, confuse, and harry the larger Marine units. Finally, the battalion commander had to commit more than one company at a time to the operations on the other side of the Tra Bong. It was on one of these multi-company operations that the battalion first tasted tragedy.

In late July, Lieutenant Colonel Hall joined his Marines in crossing the river to investigate reports of enemy activity, such as bunker building and the like. The Marines got into a pretty good fight and lost several of their own, including their first officer killed in action in Vietnam, Lt Douglas Wauchope. They also destroyed a disabled amphibian tractor to keep it from falling into enemy hands. They recrossed the river in disarray that night, and the next morning, Major General Walt flew into Chulai to personally relieve Hall of his command, and he either relieved or transferred several other officers. Almost immediately LtCol Joseph E. Muir was sent to take over.

Joe Muir was a former enlisted man, like Bull Fisher, who had came up from the ranks by dint of his own talent. In contrast to the latter, he was a slender, soft-spoken individual who inspired confidence wherever he went. His Marines, some of whom affectionately referred to him as "the Grasshopper," because he seemed to be jumping into everywhere and everything at once, held him in awe. Colonel Muir was a master at supporting arms and a believer in readiness. Within weeks any officer or staff NCO in his battalion, and many of the lesser ranks, could call in artillery, air, or naval gunfire. Moreover, their map-reading skills improved and they were turned out at all hours of the night and day to respond to drills.

THE BA GIA REGIMENT[2]

During the late 1950s, Ho Chi Minh eliminated his rivals and put his country through drastic agricultural reform to return the land to the poorest peasants.[3] His generals, primarily Vo Nguyen Giap, built the communist armed forces and fended off sabotage and commando raids from the Diem regime in the South. This harassment from the South was just that—harassment. Vietnam has always been a closed, largely agriculture society in which strangers are noticed, regarded with suspicion, and reported. Virtually all of the commandos inserted into the north were killed, captured, joined the other side, or simply disappeared.[4]

By January 1959 the Central Committee, Vietnamese Communist Party, had become impatient from waiting for its southern neighbor to collapse under its own weight. It passed Resolution 15, which stated: "The way to carry out the Vietnamese revolution in the South is through the use of violence." This set the stage for organized insurgency in the south.

In this vein, the National Liberation Front of South Vietnam was formed on December 20, 1960, to appeal to the people to unite in the fight against the Diem regime. Capitalizing on the extremely poor reputation of the French among Vietnamese of all classes, the communists invariably linked Diem's "puppet regime" with another white oppressor, the United States. They referred to the South Vietnamese president *My-Diem*, as "America's Diem."

In 1961 and 1962, the old southern Viet Minh units that had regrouped in North Vietnam after the 1954 armistice gradually infiltrated back into the South, dug up buried weapons, and recruited among young people of both genders. Marine LtCol William R. Corson, who ran one of the few successful pacification efforts during the war, asserts that the VC filled their ranks in three ways. About 40 to 42 percent of the new recruits succumbed to an intensive soft sell by the communists; another 40 to 42 percent was pressed into service; and the remainder were "walk-ins," young men who had had enough of the southern regime and sought out the VC.[5] The VC also attracted a considerable number of women, but despite many communist propaganda photos to the contrary, few were active combatants. The majority acted as auxiliaries—cooks, nurses, spies, and porters for the mostly male forces.[6]

The Bo Doi were emphatic that they did not have Chinese or Russian advisors with them in the South. Their reasoning was that they did not want to incur a blood debt. Debts of money and arms are relatively easy to repay, they argued, and if not repaid, are easily forgiven. Debts of blood are not so easily liquidated; they are debts of a far more serious nature whose price of repayment can be unacceptably high. The Vietnamese term for this is *han tu*. It literally means blood debt, although it is frequently used to mean "revenge" or even "hatred."

From the very beginning, the VC were cautioned to work with the villagers, not against them. They were instructed to emphasize nationalism, not communism, and to work with incumbent officials whenever they could. Officials, village chiefs, and the like, were in a very difficult position. Appointed by the Saigon government, they were small islands of landowners in a sea of landless peasants and were often caught between both sides in a conflict they would rather have stayed out of. The Viet Cong took violent action against those who would not support them and assassinated an estimated eleven hundred in 1959, then greatly increased that number each year in the early 1960s. The

Viet Cong cadres would obtain a consensus that such-and-such official was corrupt or an enemy of the people. At that point it was easy to eliminate the person without much public concern. The poor peasants, many of whose families had slaved for generations under an oppressive debt to the landowners, were either indifferent to these actions or glad to see them happen.[7]

On November 20, 1962, the Viet Cong 1st Infantry Regiment, consisting of three battalions, was born in Military Region V, the area around Quang Nam and Quang Ngai provinces of South Vietnam. To disguise their efforts from prying eyes and ears, the regiment was referred to in all conversations, correspondence and radio traffic as the "1st Construction Site." These soldiers were not part-time fighters in black-pajamas. The 1st Regiment was a main-force unit whose soldiers were professionals, and many of its commanders were veterans of campaigns against the French. In addition to its role as a main-force unit, the regiment took charge of the VC provincial forces, the part-time guerrillas in the Quang Ngai area.[8]

Although the Government of South Vietnam appeared to be on its last legs, anxieties about the recent landings of American troops encouraged the communists to pick up the pace. A fourth battalion of native southerners was raised in the North to become part of the 1st Viet Cong Regiment.

Dinh The Pham was typical of the 1st VC Regiment officers. He survived a life of hard campaigning and was now the deputy political officer of the 40th Battalion, 1st Viet Cong Regiment. Born in 1928, Pham had joined the army at age sixteen to fight against the Japanese. After World War II, he saw nine years of constant combat in the Viet Minh and had fought in the terrible battle against the French in Dien Bien Phu in 1954. He was one of the soldiers who had hauled artillery pieces into the hills around the French position by hand and then went on to participate in the assault on several strongpoints. It was his battalion that captured the French commander at Dien Bien Phu. Like many Viet Minh, Pham chose, or was ordered, to go North after the peace accords divided the country in order to work on what he calls "nation building."

In the early 1960s Dinh The Pham volunteered and went South with the new battalion. The communists were so certain of victory that they were choosy about whom they sent. Native southerners were preferred. At this time the Viet Cong did not have many northerners in its ranks. In the summer of 1965 the number of soldiers from North

Vietnam comprised less than 10 percent of the total fighters in the South. Married men were not, at this time, eligible. Finally, the volunteers had to be in excellent condition and health. To prove their fitness and prepare for the long trek south, they spent weeks on end carrying up to 40 kilos of dirt or sand on their backs as they walked up steep hills.

Pham, now a 2d lieutenant, would survive the war against the Americans and retire as a major. There was continual promotion for those who survived combat, because casualties were high and the army was growing. After a fierce battle everyone who was not killed was put through fresh political, military, and physical conditioning courses, and many were promoted to replace the casualties. Some of the simplest men who remained alive managed to rise through the ranks, some to quite high positions. There were colonels who were functionally illiterate but who were excellent commanders because of their experience.[9]

The regiment and its three battalions, the 40th, 60th and 90th, spent most of 1963 and early 1964 training, arming, organizing, and engaging the ARVN in small battles. They significantly increased their activities in mid-1964. Coups and counter-coups that had disrupted the government of South Vietnam since the assassination of its president, Ngo Dinh Diem, allowed the communists to move quickly to take advantage of the disorder.

The 1st Regiment's battalions fought three major actions in 1964 against ARVN forces and claimed victory in them all. In July the 60th Battalion ambushed an ARVN engineer company and destroyed most of its equipment. In August the 90th Battalion attacked a column of armored personnel carriers and destroyed several vehicles. And in October the 40th Battalion overran a company-sized ARVN camp near Tam Ky, killing or driving off the defenders and destroying two 105mm howitzers.

The early part of 1965 saw an increase in attacks on ARVN positions but not yet a regimental-size operation. The individual battalions fought two major actions in February, two more in March, and another in April 1965. Then, on April 19, the entire regiment came together and attacked the area from Vinh Huy market to Ong Trieu Bridge, where they killed or wounded 151 ARVN, destroyed 5 vehicles, and captured 51 weapons.

Following a rest of nearly six weeks, and expansion by the 45th Heavy Weapons Battalion, the regiment fought the first of a group of battles around a location, the name of which stays with it to this day, Ba Gia.

The planning directive for this series of battles was "Combat Order No. 1,"[10] a detailed nine-page document for a sustained campaign to last from May 20 until August 20, 1965. The order laid out precise missions for all elements of the regiment's battalions and supporting units. It also considered and planned for the possibility of intervention by the U.S. Marines, who had landed in Danang two months earlier and were newly ashore at Chulai. Their targets, units of the 51st ARVN Regiment, were analyzed, including estimates of mechanized equipment, artillery, and air support. The order also specified withdrawal routes. All units were ordered to complete their preparations, such as organization for combat, political motivation, and material replenishment not later than 1800 hours on May 25, 1965. The 51st ARVN Regiment was singled out for special attention because it represented a serious thorn in the side of the Viet Cong organization in Quang Tin and Quang Ngai provinces. It was part of BriGen Hoang Xuan Lam's 2d ARVN Division, which had responsibility for all the southern half of the I Corps Tactical Zone. General Lam was a particularly aggressive commander for a member of the ARVN, and his units were beginning to make some inroads into VC control of the region. The commander of the 51st ARVN Regiment, LtCol Colonel Nguyen Tho Lap, was also a dependable and aggressive ARVN commander. He constantly harried the VC in an area where they had been ascendant for many years.

As a prelude to the fight the Viet Cong sent their sappers—reconnaissance personnel—to evaluate the targets. Sappers were specially trained for this type of duty and needed to have infinite patience and nerves of steel. Organized into three- or four-man cells, they wore black or brown clothes, and each carried a pair of wire cutters but little else. They were trained to operate softly and downwind of their targets. The men walked or crawled slowly in a line at five-meter intervals. When they were some distance from the post to be reconnoitered, they moved gently and observed. Drawing near, they made full use of the topography, lying in shallow places while looking for a suitable entry to the post. After making a circle of the target, all of them assembled at a designated place to discuss their ideas. Upon deciding on an entry point they penetrated the enemy position behind their cell leader, who went in first, quietly cutting the barbed wire with his wire cutters. They moved together at intervals of approximately one meter. If they saw searchlights from the post the men would drop silently to the ground and remain motionless. As they crawled, each member moved very slowly, using both their hands and bare feet to probe the ground to locate wire that indicated that grenades or mines were planted nearby. When transiting a rice field that was muddy or full of water, the men waded noiselessly by putting the end of their toes in the water and slowly following with the rest of the foot. If dogs barked, or any unexpected obstacles appeared, they lay motionless and reported this immediately to the cell leader. Once inside the post, all the men sat together in one place and observed carefully. Then everybody withdrew, one after another, using the same route by which they had entered. They gathered again at a designated safe area to discuss their ideas. These men were talented and could move like ghosts into and out of a position. Their expertise was going to spook a lot of Americans later in the war and add to their image of invincibility.

Upon returning to their safe area the sappers were expected to know how many rows of fences encircled the post; how many entrances or exits there were; the number of pillboxes; where the automatic weapons were; how many rooms there were in the barracks; and at what time the occupants went to sleep. Each cell member reported everything he saw to the leader, who made a chart and drew up a detailed report for his superiors. [11]

After numerous such reconnaissances, the Viet Cong hit the 1st Battalion, 51st ARVN Regiment, in several places on the night of May 28-29. A company-size ARVN force guarding a bridge 1,500 meters south of Ba Gia was struck first. Then, at dawn, another company on a clearing operation to the east was attacked. A relief force under the command of the battalion commander piled into five vehicles and went out to help the company in the east. By this time the VC had broken contact at the bridge. The ARVN commander ordered one of the platoons from the company at the bridge to return to reinforce at Ba Gia and the other two platoons to join him en route to the besieged unit to the east. The 60th and 90th battalions of the 1st VC Regiment[12] ambushed the relief column and the ARVN lost radio contact with the outside.[13] Among the members of this force were three American advisors, who were reported as missing in action and feared dead along with the battalion commander and his command group.[14]

The 1st Battalion, 51st ARVN Regiment, reported light casualties at the scene, but had an astounding three hundred men were missing in action. At mid-morning on May 29, the 39th ARVN Ranger Battalion;

the 2d Battalion, 51st ARVN Regiment; and the 3d Vietnamese Marine Corps (VNMC) Battalion (VNMC) were committed to the operation.[15]

The 39th Ranger Battalion quickly became surrounded and lost control of the situation. Its CO and operations officer were badly wounded and the executive officer was killed in action. A U.S. advisor, Capt Christopher O'Sullivan, was also killed, and the battalion intelligence officer found himself in command. Casualties were so heavy that by the end of the operation the rangers would have only one effective company. Major General Nguyen Chanh Thi, the ARVN commander for all of I Corps, asked for a U.S. Marine battalion and two Vietnamese airborne battalions. He got neither, but he did get some Marine Corps helicopter and fixed-wing support.

To reduce the effectiveness of further ARVN reinforcement, Ba Gia again came under attack by artillery, mortars, automatic weapons, and rifle fire. The Vietnamese Marine battalion was hit in the night and suffered sixty casualties. The missing U.S. advisors who had been with the relief force were picked up the next day and survived the operation.[16]

The 1st Battalion, 51st ARVN Regiment, was badly mauled. Of approximately 500 men when the battle began, 392 were killed or missing and 446 individual weapons and 90 crew-served weapons were lost to the enemy.[17]

The Viet Cong also suffered grievous losses. The 40th Battalion was particularly hard hit. It began the operation with four companies. One of them, the 361st, was completely wiped out as it led the assault with human-wave tactics. In this company, every one of the 95 officers and men were killed or wounded except Mien, the political officer. All three company commanders in the battalion were killed in action. [18]

One of the reasons for high losses was erroneous information given to the 361st Company by its own reconnaissance people. The sappers claimed that there was only a platoon defending the position the company was to attack. The defending force was actually a company, and it decimated the VC ranks. The sappers who provided the faulty information were put in jail and their weapons and equipment were taken from them.[19]

Approximately 220 ARVN who were among the missing were captured by the VC and taken to a remote camp to be reindoctrinated. They were taught to hate the Americans, speak ill of the South Vietnamese regime, and praise North Vietnam. They were also taught to dig communications trenches, to make obstacles, and to attack fortified positions. Their training was unrelenting. It lasted from 0430 until 2130 daily, and covered a variety of subjects, including attacking with satchel charges, attacking communications trenches, attacking houses, defenses against aircraft and artillery, camouflage, and movement.[20]

Duong Van Phouc was one of these men. The 22-year-old had been a member of the 3d Platoon, 3d Company, 1st Battalion, 51st ARVN Regiment. After capture he was assigned to the 40th VC Battalion along with other former ARVN to replace the casualties at Ba Gia, and he was to fight on the VC side on Starlite. In the confusion of that battle he managed to detach himself from his new unit on August 22 and surrender back to the ARVN along with this weapon.[21]

For the three days of combat that ended on May 31, 1965, the 1st VC Regiment was cited and awarded the Honor Banner with the inscription "Loyal to the Party, Dutiful to the People, and First in the Victory of Ba Gia."[22] To this day, 1st Viet Cong Regiment veterans of the battle call themselves the Ba Gia Regiment and consider themselves to be the elite of their army.

The 1st Regiment hit Ba Gia again five weeks later. At 0300 on July 5, once again using human wave tactics, the 1st VC Regiment overran the 1st Battalion, 51st ARVN Regiment, once more. Of the 257 ARVN soldiers at the beginning of the battle, only 40 were left when relief came. The remainder and a U.S. Army advisor, Capt William Eisenbraun, were missing. Captain Eisenbraun's body was found the next day and Army SFC Henry Musa, initially among the missing in the first battle of Ba Gia, was also dead. The VC captured numerous weapons, including two 105mm howitzers and several hundred 105mm rounds. The guns were last seen being towed from the area by jeeps. Among the missing ARVN were fourteen artillerymen who knew how to service and fire these weapons. For years the Americans worried about the artillery pieces and the use the VC might make of them. Lieutenant Colonel Trung, one of the Bo Doi, told the author in September 1999 that the weapons were buried in the hills to the west but never used by the Viet Cong. The ARVN eventually found and recaptured them but apparently never told the Americans.

Allied aircraft flew 110 sorties in support of the operation on July 5 and 6. One U.S. helicopter was shot down killing the copilot, CWO Allen Holt. The VC kept up mortar and harassing fires throughout the next two days and then again withdrew as Ba Gia was reinforced.[23]

Once more the VC paid for their victory in blood. The 364th Company of the 40th Battalion had been re-designated the 361st to replace the company wiped out in the first battle of Ba Gia. The 361st was once more named to lead the attack and was once more destroyed. Only the political officer who had escaped from the first battle, and one other unnamed soldier, survived. The other companies also sustained heavy losses, particularly among the officers.[24]

For two more months, the regiment planned and executed operations in Quang Ngai Province, keeping military pressure on their foes, capturing weapons, and eliminating strategic hamlets. Finally, in early August, the Ba Gia Regiment went to ground in rest areas. Two battalions, the 40th and 60th, and the regimental headquarters stayed in the coastal Van Tuong area while the other two battalions encamped about 15 kilometers south and slightly further inland. The regiment not only required rest, it needed to replenish its ranks, and it expected resupply to come in from the sea.

The regimental commander was Le Huu Tru, who had commanded the 803d Regiment of the 324th Division in 1954 at Dien Bien Phu. His political officer was Nguyen Dinh Trong, who had held the same post in the city of Danang in the war against the French. Nguyen Xuan Phung commanded the 60th Battalion, and his political officer was Nguyen To. Duong Ba Loi headed the 40th Battalion, and his political officers were Le Lung and his assistant Dinh The Pham.

Political officers were assigned at every level from the high command down through at least the company level. Their duties were overseeing the morale and motivation of the other members of their unit. To become a political officer was a great honor. They were selected from among those party members who displayed a great deal of knowledge about why they were fighting, demonstrated outstanding ability to influence others, and showed exemplary courage on the battlefield. They acted as father, elder brother, and confessor as well as political teachers. Because of their past actions they were regarded with a great deal of respect by the ordinary soldiers. They were instrumental not only in encouraging bravery on the battlefield but in reminding the soldiers to treat the people well and to win them over to the cause.[25] Their propaganda was laced with tales of cruel landlords and repressive officials, something nearly all the soldiers had personal experience with. They also played the anti-colonial theme over and over; only these days the subject of their scorn was the Americans in lieu of the French. The political officers composed simple poems, slogans, and songs that were easy to understand and memorize. Conversation and self-criticism was mandatory. Everyone, including officers, was required to participate, and their confessional was held out in the open for all to see and hear. A form of absolution was passed along to those who satisfied the others with their sincerity and willingness to repent. This led even the lowest private to feel that he had a role in the decision-making process. In late 20th century business management this is known as "empowerment."

During the period immediately after a major battle or campaign the Viet Cong customarily gathered their commanders in a central location to discuss further battle plans. At these times the units were left under the command of the political officers. This was the case with the Ba Gia Regiment in early August 1965. Le Huu Tru, the regimental commander; Luu Thanh Duc, his deputy; and the battalion commanders left for a secret location in the dense highlands west of Chulai for a conference. Command of the unit was in the hands of Nguyen Dinh Trong and the other political officers.

The first thing the two battalions of the regiment did when they reached the Van Tuong peninsula was to fortify and camouflage. Their survival against the French, and now the Americans, depended on their being able to hide well. Every man carried a small shovel he had a lot of practice using. Viet Cong units threw up bunkers and dug trenches and tunnels with astonishing speed. Their camouflage discipline was superb. Most Americans, their faith firmly anchored in firepower and technology, could not be bothered with camouflage at all. When they did anything it usually consisted of sticking a few branches of whatever they could find in their helmets, or around their positions, and then not change them no matter what the circumstances.

The Viet Minh and their successors, the Viet Cong, had learned that to avoid enemy technology, particularly air power, it was necessary to master the art of camouflage. Even when the VC thought they were in safe areas they would skillfully camouflage anything that might reveal their position. They camouflaged their pith helmets, and on his back each man carried a bamboo or wire frame for placement of concealing articles. As they passed through varying types of terrain they would immediately change the foliage to match that of their surroundings. For example, if they passed from a light to a dark green area or to the brown area of a ripe crop, they would stop and religiously replace the camouflage. When aircraft flew overhead they most often avoided detection simply by remaining motionless.

The men of the 1st Regiment were not expecting to fight a battle at Van Tuong. They looked forward to resting and supplementing their grim field rations with some vegetables and maybe a little fish or pork. They expected to engage in social and cultural activities with the population of this area, which had always been receptive to their cause. Most of them were young in years, not much different in average age, about nineteen, from their enemy. But they had just finished a hard campaign, so even the greenest among them had far more combat experience than their adversaries. They endured constant fear, poor diet, overwork, and filth. They knew the terrors of rushing into combat and the sorrow of mourning slain comrades. Unlike the Marines, they did not return home at the end of thirteen months. Only death or victory limited their combat tours. The best they had to look forward to was a few weeks of improved rations, singing, listening to guitars, and flirting with the local girls.

* * *

The Viet Cong were already taking the measure of their American opponents. An evaluation, dated July 3, 1965, said the following:

American strong points

- They have reached the training level of an expeditionary force

- Armed with modern weapons, lighter than French expeditionary forces, they have quick transportation, quick movement, have capability of quick reinforcement, thanks to vehicles, aircraft, boats

- Usually concentrated by groups

Weak points compared with French

- No spirit of combat; afraid of guerrillas; always rely on modern weapons, so they lose initiative and self-confidence (when in contact, they call fire for support and reinforcement); sometimes artillery must conduct fire support for the whole period of operation.

- Lack of combat experience, just know combat in theory only (through field manuals). Moreover, on a strange terrain, they usually walk in the open, bewildered like ducks (we say that American troops are most opportune targets for guerrillas).

- Much effort required for messing; and water. Food must be supplied for each meal by helicopters. When moving to any place they must use helicopters and artillery fire support, so objective will always be disclosed, bringing good opportunity for guerrilla follow up.

- Cannot undergo long and hard operations. When operating far from base, about seven kilometers, must use vehicles.

- Not able to bear local weather and climate, so troops will fall ill.

- Defensive positions sometimes well organized but they are slow to get that way. In one instance it took ten days to organize defenses and thirty to install mines.

- They do not know the terrain well.

- They run slowly."

The evaluation ended with the statement, "Americans came to South Vietnam, killed, robbed and raped women, and invoked much blood debt with our people."[26]

The VC also claimed to be able to tell Marine operational objectives by the way they moved, their supply activities, and their prep fires.

PART II

CHAPTER 5

THE BATTLE

THE ENEMY THREATENS

It is axiomatic of military planning that one must take into account an enemy's capabilities rather than his intentions. For several months allied intelligence estimated that the enemy was capable of bringing as many as two full regiments down from the nearby Annamite Cordillera, the ragged and overgrown mountain chain that runs most of the length of Vietnam's interior. These mountains run southward out of China and their peaks average over 5,000 feet. A heavily jungled spur comes to within ten kilometers of the Chulai plain. Hidden by the foliage were numerous trails that could allow the enemy fairly easy access to the Chulai area and provide escape routes as well. To mass two regiments of men in one area would, on the one hand, present grave risks to an enemy commander. If discovered by the ARVN and Americans, such a force might be severely mauled by superior allied firepower. On the other hand, the VC capability presented a serious threat to the Marine air base.

For weeks the after the battle of Ba Gia, the 2d ARVN Division looked for the enemy with no success. It was thought they had gone back toward the dense hills. As we have seen, they moved in a bit closer to Chulai and were resting from the Ba Gia campaign.

The heads-up analysis of the 3d Marine Division intelligence section headed up by Maj Charles Williamson and his assistant Capt Mike Dominguez picked this up. Their order-of-battle information began to show patterns of movement eastward by the 1st Viet Cong Regiment.

Colonel Leo J. Dulacki, General Walt's intelligence officer (G2) explained the efforts of the Williamson-Dominguez team like this, "Early in August we began receiving countless low-level reports from numerous intelligence collection organizations concerning the movement of the 1st VC Regiment. The sources for most of these reports were of doubtful reliability and, indeed, many were contradictory, nevertheless, it was decided to plot all of the hundreds of reported movements, regardless of credibility, on a map, and an interesting picture developed. When the many aberrations were discounted, it appeared that the 1st VC Regiment was, in fact, moving towards Chulai although most of the intelligence experts, including the ARVN and the U.S. Army's I Corps Advisory Group, discounted such a possibility. I briefed Col Edwin Simmons, III MAF G-3, on what appeared to be developing and suggested the consideration, if further indicators developed, of an offensive operation in the area south of Chulai."[1]

Acting on this intelligence, the 4th Marines conducted a one-battalion operation alongside the 51st ARVN Regiment to search for the enemy south of the Tra Bong River. Codenamed Thunderbolt, the operation lasted for two days, August 6 and 7, and extended 7,000 meters south of the river and west of Route 1. The ARVN and Marines found little sign of a major VC force and encountered only scattered enemy activity. The Marines suffered more from the 110-degree heat than from a human enemy. Nevertheless, Col James McClanahan, the CO of the 4th Marines, felt that the operation was a useful exercise in command and control.[2] A week later the pace quickened.

*   *   *

Captain Cal Morris, commander of Mike Company, 3/3, was running combat patrols south of the river on August 15 and 16 when his Marines encountered and killed some of the enemy. The dead soldiers wore khaki uniforms, not the black-pajamas typical of the VC village militia the Marines had previously seen. And they were better armed. One had a rocket propelled grenade (RPG) launcher, an armor- and bunker-busting weapon, which was rarely seen at this point in the war. The others were armed with what appeared to be automatic shoulder weapons of Chinese Communist manufacture. These were strange to the Marines, and they could not be identified at the company level. Captain Morris afterward thought that they might have been AK47s, which were to become ubiquitous later in the war. The enemy corpses and weapons were quickly evacuated to the rear for evaluation.

Also on August 15 the 1st Marine Radio Battalion located what appeared to be the 1st VC Regiment headquarters near the village of Van Tuong. The Marines intercepted radio message traffic of a unit they believed to be the 1st VC Regiment and located it with direction finding equipment. This information was quickly confirmed by further intercepts and was passed to Major Williamson's intelligence team, which immediately processed it and notified General Walt's III MAF staff.

THE DEFECTOR

The same day, MajGen Nguyen Chanh Thi, the ARVN commander of the I Corps Military Region, had urgent news for General Walt. A captured VC, Thi told the Marine commanding general, revealed that the notorious 1st VC Regiment was massing south of the Tra Bong River, near the village of Van Tuong, on the Van Tuong peninsula, in preparation for an assault on the Marine base at Chulai. Numbering about two thousand troops, this force was to attack and destroy the main air station facilities and aircraft while local guerrilla forces pinned the defenders in place with relatively minor but noisy and potentially dangerous actions. The defector was a seventeen-year-old named Vo Thao, who had been abducted by the VC during Tet, the Lunar New Year festival, in 1965. After a few weeks training Thao had been assigned to the 40th Battalion of the 1st Regiment. Typifying many Vietnamese, he had relatives on both sides of the fight. His paternal uncle was a member of the VC, three other uncles worked for the ARVN or the Americans, and his stepfather was an ARVN sergeant.

When his Viet Cong commander refused permission for Thao to visit his family, he had filled out false leave papers and deserted.[3]

General Thi told Walt that he thought this was the best, the most reliable, information he had received about the enemy in the entire Vietnam War. Walt considered his reaction and, apprehensive about leaks to the enemy, asked General Thi to not share this information with other Vietnamese commanders. Walt then set out for Chulai to discuss the situation with his commanders on the ground there.[4]

General Nguyen Chanh Thi's information was only partially correct. Part of the regiment, the 40th and 60th battalions, and elements of the 45th Weapons Battalion, were at Van Tuong. The remaining units were about fifteen kilometers further south. And the VC force was not preparing for a regimental-size attack on Chulai. The enemy commanders had already decided to limit attacks on the Marine base to small, highly mobile, and suicidal sapper attacks. At this time, the enemy commanders were away at their meeting in the mountains west of Chulai to discuss how they might draw the Americans out from their bases and reduce the effectiveness of American supporting arms and mobility.

THE OPTIONS

On August 16 Walt held a conference at Chulai with the assistant division commander, BriGen Frederick Karch; Col James McClanahan, commander of the 4th Marines; Col Oscar "Peat" Peatross, commanding officer of Regimental Landing Team 7 (RLT-7); and a few staff members. He outlined the situation and emphasized that the data he had was very sensitive and that the information should not go below battalion level. After sharing the intelligence, the general reviewed his options. Walt was faced with the decision of trying to preempt a possible attack on the air base with an attack on the Viet Cong, or defending. The former course of action would strip most of the forces from Chulai, rendering it vulnerable to attack. The latter would allow the enemy time to build up his logistics base, thereby strengthening himself for the attack at a later date. General Walt knew he was going to have to fight the VC sooner or later and he decided to do so on his own terms by carrying the fight to the enemy.[5]

After counting the forces and responsibilities within his area he did not believe he could spare any troops from Danang. The most he could count on for an operation were two Marine battalions, and he thought that they should be 3/3 and 2/4. Having decided that, he would have to scrape up other resources to increase his chances of success on the battlefield. In the doctrine of the 1960s it was felt that the attacker needed a "combat power" ratio of 3:1 over a defender to conduct a successful operation. Two Marine battalions attacking a two-thousand-man enemy force would make the fighting troops on the ground nearly even in manpower. Walt would have to get his "combat power" from his supporting arms. The general looked at Colonel Peatross and said, "Peat, you are the only one available [to run the operation]. I know all your gear is out on the beach because you just landed yesterday."[6]

Peatross recalled later that Walt gave him the option of going or not going, and told him (Peatross) that if he didn't go the operation would have to be called off. There is no evidence that two aggressive Marines like Peatross and Walt, both former Marine Raiders, ever thought that *not* going was a viable option. Nevertheless, Peatross did say that he wanted to talk to the battalion commanders who would be involved. Walt gave Peatross another option, that of using the 1st Battalion, 7th Marines (1/7), one of Peatross's own battalions, for the operation, but he recommended that Peatross allow them to continue to relieve 3/3 in the defensive perimeter at Chulai, because that is what they were doing anyway, and then use 3/3 for the operation. Peatross was fond of quoting General of the Army Omar Bradley, who once said that 90 percent of success in battle was knowing one's subordinates. Peatross was very familiar with the commanders of 3/3 and 2/4. He had known Lieutenant Colonel Muir since the latter came through the Basic School at Quantico as a lieutenant and again at Camp Pendleton, when Peatross first took over the 7th Marines. He and Lieutenant Colonel Fisher had been on Iwo Jima together. In fact, Peatross had been acquainted with both of these officers longer than he had known his own battalion commanders.[7] After speaking with Muir and Fisher, and flying with them over the objective area, Peatross confirmed that he was ready to go. He asked that Walt try to get Battalion Landing Team 3/7, from Admiral Sharp, the commander-in-chief, Pacific (CinCPac), as regimental reserve. This battalion had been designated the Special Landing Force (SLF) and was the theater reserve for the entire Pacific region. Walt agreed, and Admiral Sharp immediately approved the request from his headquarters in Hawaii. The problem was that the unit was in the Philippines.[8]

* * *

Peatross's equipment was indeed on the beach, but his regiment was landing in Vietnam administratively. He had been told at Camp Pendleton, California, to be prepared to land tactically, then, once he got to Vietnam, the 3d Marine Division told him to land administratively. So all of his equipment was stacked up on the beach. Landing administratively meant that priority was given to making maximum use of hold space on the ships when loading and on getting the supplies and equipment off the ship in the most expeditious manner regardless of the order in which it came off. Landing tactically meant that the ships were combat loaded with combat equipment more readily available at the top of the holds, so it could be off-loaded in the presumed order a unit engaged with the enemy would need. Because RLT-7 landed administratively, all of its equipment was arrayed on the beach in a very jumbled manner.[9]

COLONEL PEATROSS

Peat Peatross and his regiment were new to Vietnam, but the colonel himself was a seasoned combat veteran of two previous wars. A trim, bespectacled southerner, with accompanying accent, Peatross looked more like the textile engineer he had trained to be at the University of North Carolina than the war hero he was. Oscar Peatross had been a member of LtCol Evans F. Carlson's famed Marine Raiders during World War II. Carlson's men, whose ranks included James Roosevelt, FDR's son, made a daring raid on the Japanese-held island of Makin in the Gilbert Island chain early in the war. Makin was well within the confines of that area of the Pacific the Japanese had rapidly overrun in the early days of the war. The numerically superior enemy force was caught completely off guard when Colonel Carlson and his small Raider unit landed at night by rubber boat from submarines. Peatross's party, tossed up on a beach well away from the main body, found itself right in the middle of a much larger Japanese unit and fought its way to join up with the other Raiders. His advance was hotly contested but successful for the Marines, who killed dozens of the enemy. For his leadership in the battle Peatross was awarded the Navy Cross Medal, the nation's second highest combat award.[10] Peatross participated in other Pacific campaigns and later had commanded a battalion under then-Col Lew Walt in Korea.

RLT-7

RLT-7 arrived in Okinawa from California in June 1965. Beginning in May 1965, it was alerted for movement to Vietnam and had begun getting intelligence briefings on a daily basis. This continued all the way across the Pacific and throughout the stay Okinawa. During July, the colonel and his staff visited all the Marine areas in Vietnam to gain familiarity with the enemy and the problems of fighting in Vietnam.[11] On August 8, the unit embarked aboard Amphibious Squadron 7 (PhibRon-7) for the leg of its voyage to Vietnam. The force consisted of the RLT headquarters, BLT 1/7 and BLT 3/9.[12]

The Marines of RLT-7 were well trained according to the doctrine of the day. And they were well prepared for coordination with their air and naval counterparts, both Navy and Marine. Training on Marine tactical doctrine on the use of helicopters was particularly important, because it was still being developed. Marines had used helicopters in combat as far back as Korea, and in Vietnam they had three and a half years of experience with the Shufly advisory operation. But they had yet to fly large numbers of Marines into combat in accordance with the practices they had developed over the previous dozen years. Starlite would be the first big test.[13]

En route to Vietnam the composition of the landing team changed again when 3/9 was diverted to Danang and detached from the RLT. Thus RLT-7 arrived in Chulai on August 14 with only its headquarters and Battalion Landing Team 1/7.[14]

For Starlite, the units were once more juggled. In the end RLT-7 consisted of 3/3, 2/4, and the RLT staff. These units were alerted on the afternoon of August 16. The newly landed 1/7, under LtCol James B. Kelly, had been designated to take over the defensive positions of Chulai from 3/3 and was already moving into place.[15]

THE PLAN

The decision made and the units chosen, planning began in earnest. The first task was to figure out a method of attack. A helicopter landing by all the forces involved was out of the question because there were not enough aircraft to lift both battalions into the objective area. Even if there had been ample choppers, Peatross's force would still need amphibious shipping to bring ashore tanks and other heavy equipment, as well as to provide the logistic support to keep the assault rolling.

A ground attack was considered but rejected. There were not enough trucks available to move sufficient numbers of Marines rapidly down Highway 1. Moving them overland on foot would eliminate the important element of surprise. The Van Tuong peninsula lay about 12,000 meters from Highway 1, which was the only real land supply artery. The Marines would have to march overland to the objective area on minor roads and trails, and there would have been no way to protect the communications routes on Route 1, and from there to the objective area. Attacking from the air and from the sea at the same time would remove these difficulties and preserve the surprise factor.

Besides his experience with Joe Muir and Bull Fisher, Peatross's long acquaintance with General Walt expedited the planning and coordination between the division staff and the RLT-7 headquarters. Of similar advantage to Peatross and his staff was that they worked together previously with the amphibious commander, Captain McKinney, his staff, and the same ships on Operation Silver Lance in California only five months earlier. This relationship undoubtedly contributed to McKinney's willingness to proceed with the operation on oral instructions.[16]

Later on August 16, just prior to dusk, the two battalion commanders; Colonel Peatross; Capt Dave Ramsey, the 3/3 S-3 (operations officer); and Maj Andy Comer made a hurried helicopter reconnaissance right over the objective area in General Walt's personal UH-1E Huey helicopter. They looked at landing beaches, and Lieutenant Colonel Fisher searched for possible helicopter landing zones (LZs). As they flew over the objective area a few unidentified Vietnamese peeked up at them from some of the remote wooded areas. The flight was hurried so as to be less obvious as to its intent. The Marines observed that the proposed battleground was rolling country, about 75 percent of it cultivated, and elsewhere there was thick scrub from three to six feet high. Hedgerows, many of bamboo that ranged in height from six to nearly a hundred feet, compartmentalized the area. The hedgerows marked field and village boundaries and were often too thick to move through easily. The beaches were sandy and narrow, but in a few cases the dunes advance inland as far as 2,000 meters.[17]

THE ENEMY IS WARNED

The brevity and apparent casualness of the reconnaissance flight did not fool the Viet Cong. Based on the activity their scouts observed at Chulai they figured the Americans were going to attack the Van Tuong peninsula. The French writer Bernard Fall made an important statement about the enormous intelligence advantage Giap's forces had. He wrote about the war with the French, but his warning was also applicable in the war with the Americans. "It must be understood that practically all troop movements in Indochina took place in a fishbowl. Since practically no troop movements took place at night for fear of costly ambushes, even the smallest movement of troops, tanks or aircraft was immediately noted by the population and brought to the attention of communist agents. Thus, the only effect of tactical surprise, which could be achieved, was that of speed in executing a movement, rather than in the concealment of the movement itself. The communists, therefore, nearly always had a fairly accurate idea of French forces in any given sector and knew how many of these troops could be made available for mobile operations. Since the number of troops required to protect a given number of miles of communications lines also was a known constant, it was almost mathmatically possible to calculate the maximum depth of the French penetration and its duration."[18]

In the case of Operation Starlite, the VC determined the objective but seriously underestimated the speed with which the American Marines could mount the attack. They also misjudged the manner of attack.

They had an additional problem in that their regimental commander, Le Huu Tru, and his assistant, Lu Van Duc, were not present. These men were at their conference in the dense hills due west of Chulai.

The purpose of this conference, convened after the VC victory at Ba Gia, was to determine how to deal with the Marines at Chulai. Other than the assertions of Vo Thao, the seventeen-year-old defector, there is no evidence that the 1st VC Regiment ever seriously contemplated a full-scale attack on the Chulai base. The Viet Cong had never fought the Marines in this type of assault before.

Inasmuch as the commanders were absent, it fell to Political Officer Nguyen Dinh Trong and his assistant, Hu Tuong, to meet the Americans. Among the things under consideration was the question of whether or not to bring up the 45th and 90th battalions from their positions fifteen kilometers south Van Tuong. Trong and Tuong delayed this decision until the battle was already joined, and at that point it was too late. In the meantime the 40th and 60th battalions were fully alerted and going through drills to meet various contingencies.

The VC officers disagreed as to the direction from which the attack would come. They considered three possibilities: The Americans would attack south over the Tra Bong River; overland from Route 1; or by helicopter. At this point in the war they were not fully appreciative of the ability of Marines to project power ashore through amphibious operations, so they fatally discounted the idea of a landing from the sea. After much discussion they finally agreed that the enemy did not have enough helicopters to mount an effective assault from the air. So their immediate preparation concentrated on overland attacks from the north or west. They felt confident that they could meet the Marines on VC terms. That is, they could ambush and inflict casualties on the Americans and then fade away as they had in the past.

RLT PLANNING CONTINUES

A tent was erected on the beach at Chulai on the morning of August 17 for another briefing of the staff of Amphibious Squadron 7 and Regimental Landing Team 7. The beaches in the landing area had been surveyed by a Navy underwater demolition team both before and after the Marines landed at Chulai the previous May. Two of them appeared suitable for landing the amphibious force. The two are about 4,000 meters apart, and both have sandy bottoms. Other than that, they differ.

After flying over the area the commanders discussed the characteristics of each beach: gradient, width, shelter afforded, tides, terrain inland, etc. Finally, Peatross and McKinney agreed upon the southern beach, near the small fishing village of An Cuong 1. From there the VC could be driven toward Chulai and into an area in which a blocking position could readily be established by a unit that would march overland from the base. The selected area was named Green Beach. The rejected beach was farther north, at the village of Phuoc Thuan 3, and situated midway between two headlands about a mile apart. Although low tide on the August 18 was to be just before H-hour, the rise and fall of the tide, surf conditions, and beach gradient at An Cuong 1 were thought to be satisfactory for an amphibious landing at any time of the day.

Then there were the helicopter landing zones. In war-fighting theory, it is desirable to land helicopters in the rear of the enemy front line, but in Vietnam there were no such lines. The Viet Cong either did not defend at all, or they defended the entire perimeter of whatever they occupied, and there were usually trees and houses within the defended area. The landing zones would have to be large enough to accommodate the helicopters and far enough inland to isolate the targeted VC units from others outside the objective area. They would also have to be far enough inland to permit the use of supporting arms by the water-borne force during its advance from the beach. Moreover, they could not be in heavily populated areas, because it would be necessary to use naval gunfire and other supporting arms to prepare them. For the same reasons they could not be located too close to one another. The three landing zones selected ran roughly north to south and were about 2,000 meters apart.

While Muir and Comer discussed the beach areas, Bull Fisher pointed decisively at the map and asserted, "I'll land here, here, and here," as he designated the helicopter landing zones for his assault companies. He named the LZs, from north to south, Red, White, and Blue.[19]

The plan, having been agreed upon by the commanders, was coordinated and put to paper by Peatross's operations officer, Maj Elmer Snyder, who worked his staff all night.

Lieutenant Colonel Lloyd Childers, whose helicopter squadron was responsible for much for the support, was not invited to the meeting because of the extreme security concerns. Instead, he got a brief and operationally useless fragmentary order. As a result, his

HMM-361 was deprived of information that would have made it more effective. For one thing, he did not know that the 7th Marines command group would be running the operation. He thought, logically, it would be the 4th Marines, which had occupied the Chulai enclave for three months. Thus, no one thought to obtain the 7th Marines radio frequencies for the operation. Until this was sorted out, the aviators and ground forces would have to relay their traffic through the 4th Marines CP. This would considerably slow operations at critical times.

3/3 HUSTLES TO GET READY

While the two battalion commanders continued to meet with Colonel Peatross and his staff, Maj Andy Comer hustled back to 3/3 command post to get the battalion moving. D-day was set for the next morning, August 18, and H-hour was coordinated with sunrise, 0630. There was not a moment to lose. Things went somewhat easier for the battalion as it had already had completed contingency planning for an operation in this area. Even with this advantage, it was a stretch to get the troops ready and loaded aboard the transports on the afternoon of the August 17. Captain Bruce Webb's India Company, 3/3, was recalled from a company operation in the field and dispatched directly to the amphibious ships. It would be in the first wave of the assault. The other first-wave company was Capt Jay Doub's Kilo, 3/3.

APPLICATION OF DOCTRINE

Peatross's plan was to isolate, then destroy, the enemy. To insure this isolation, all elements of RLT-7—those landing in the helicopter landing zones and those coming across the beach—would have to link up during the early afternoon of D-day. They wanted the VC to think there was only one escape route—to the north. That route was to be blocked by a rifle company infiltrated into place the night before the operation began.

Commodore William McKinney directed his ships to be anchored 2,000 meters offshore at first light. Muir's battalion had been chosen to be the amphibious assault group simply because it was located closest to the beach and was therefore easiest to embark.

The operational plans were based on established amphibious doctrine, developed in the 1930s and honed to near perfection in World War II. The big difference was the helicopter element. The Marines and Navy had practiced combined helicopter and amphibious landings time after time but never before against an armed enemy. The Navy called the guiding document NWP 22(a) Doctrine for Amphibious Operations, and the Marine Corps referred to the same publication as LFM-01. Plans were completed quickly because the units were so well trained in this doctrine and had practiced it religiously.

Most of the Marines in both battalions had done this together for more than two years, albeit in non-hostile settings. The officers and men of 3/3, for example, had been aboard more than twenty amphibious ships long enough to have a meal. They had internalized the five-paragraph combat order that leaders issue to their troops, and gave them without having to think about them very much. To most of them this was just the way they made their living; there was no sense that this operation would be different from what they practiced many, many times.

The landing force was fortunate to have three ships in the area that could provide naval gunfire. They were the cruiser USS *Galveston* (CLG 3) with six 5-inch and six 6-inch guns; and two destroyers, the USS *Orleck* (DD 886) and USS *Prichett* (DD 561), each with four 5-inch guns.[20]

Their captains, as is normal, did not take part in the planning conferences, but they were professionals who had been indoctrinated in the art of naval gunfire support.

Equipment and supplies were sorted and staged on the beach and at helicopter staging points on August 17. By 1400 that day men, supplies, and equipment were being embarked in the ships of PhibRon-7. Colonel Peatross and the headquarters of RLT-7 went aboard the USS *Bayfield* (APA 33), Commodore McKinney's flagship. The BLT 3/3 headquarters, plus India and Kilo companies, went aboard the USS *Cabildo* (LSD 16), and Lima Company was embarked in the USS *Vernon County* (LST 1161).

The commanders and staff got little sleep as planning and coordination continued well into the night. The task force weighed anchor and sailed due east at 2200. All an observer on shore could tell was that the American ships moved east over the horizon. Well out of enemy sight and under the cover of darkness, the ships turned in order to reach the objective area just in time for the assault to begin. A makeshift armored force of both flame and gun tanks from both the 1st and 3d Tank battalions and Ontos from the 1st Anti-tank Battalion boarded several landing craft, utility (LCUs), which sailed independently towards the amphibious objective area, timing their arrival to coincide with that of the troop transports.[21]

As they loaded aboard ship that afternoon the troops, who were completely uninformed, were pretty much unconcerned; they played grab-ass aboard the ship and didn't think the operation was going to be much different from all their previous "long walks in the sun."

Lieutenant Burt Hinson was on the beach loading his platoon, when Staff Sergeant Bradley from the battalion supply section asked if he had plenty of rounds for his .45-caliber automatic pistol. Hinson wasn't even sure how much ammunition he had, because his skipper, Jay Doub, didn't think that officers needed weapons anyway. They should be too busy directing their troops to fire weapons. In any event, Bradley talked Hinson into taking several extra loaded magazines of .45-caliber ammo.

There were no sleeping quarters on the ships for most of the Marines, so they rested as best they could among their gear and the amphibian tractors (amtracs) and the landing craft. Many reflected on the sun as it sank over Vietnam and wondered what they would see in its early morning rays when they hit the beach the next day. The religious among them prayed, others wrote letters home, and some just smoked and talked with their comrades.

That night they lined up for a hot supper of chili and rice. Chili and rice does not sound like much of a meal, but the Marines were grateful. It was a welcome relief from the canned fare on which they subsisted for the three previous months.

They were assigned to amtracs just like the diagrams they used in schools would indicate and as they were trained. The Marines of 3/3 had been doing this, together, for a long time. They knew the drill.

The ships weighed anchor at 0200, set a course of 70 degrees, east-northeast, and sailed from the pick-up point. At a little after 0400, after the Marines had eaten a breakfast of eggs and pancakes, all hands were called to general quarters and the ships reversed course. They arrived off the objective area shortly after 0500, dropped anchor in seven fathoms of water a mile-and-a-half offshore, and prepared to launch their assault boats.[22]

ALARM!

Although the VC did not expect the Marines from the sea, here they were! As soon as the ships were spotted, messages rang over phone lines and messengers hot-footed around the 1st Viet Cong Regiment area to inform the VC that the Americans were not only coming in from the sea but they were coming in *now*, much sooner than expected. The ships were off a beach that was less than four kilometers from the 1st VC regimental command post.

The Viet Cong immediately reacted. Duong Hong Minh was sent down to the beach as quickly as he could get there to set up and prepare to set off a command-detonated mine against the American force. Phan Tan Huan, a staff officer, organized a small force that moved into a blocking position between the beach and the command post. His mission was to fight a delaying action, if necessary, to slow the enemy down and permit the 1st Viet Cong Regiment command post to relocate to a more secure position.

THE ANVIL MOVES INTO PLACE

Captain Cal Morris had moved his Mike Company, 3/3, into place the night before. Morris was not a physically imposing figure, but he was tough and well-liked by his men and his peers. Mike Company was to be the blocking force, the anvil, in this operation, and it would set in along a ridgeline to the north of the objective area. The amphibious landing force, that is the other companies in 3/3, and the helicopter landing force, Bull Fisher's 2/4, were the hammers that were expected to drive the enemy toward Morris's Marines, so they could complete the job.

The Mike Company Marines bedded down about dusk on the August 17. They awakened at 2230, saddled up, and trekked down to the Tra Bong River. From that point they marched down the beach about two kilometers and then loaded aboard amtracs to cross the river to the peninsula. Then they marched inland until they reached their blocking position. It was a very dark night, and the only way they could keep in contact was to march one behind the other with the man behind holding on to the pack of the man in front. They would have been easy targets for an alert enemy. Luckily, they were not spotted.

Mike Company reached its objective at around 0230 without incident and turned to digging in. A battery of six 107mm howtars from 3/12 were heli-lifted into Mike Company's position at dawn to provide close artillery support.

Among the Marines that set up the blocking force that night was Lt Bill Krulak, one of Lieutenant General Krulak's sons, who was a platoon commander in Mike Company.

By daylight, as the amphibious assault force was about to cross the beach, Mike Company was ready.

THE MAGNIFICENT BASTARDS

The 2/4 commander, Joseph R. "Bull" Fisher, was one of the most colorful battalion commanders in the Corps. He was a large Marine, 6'3" or so, and about 220 pounds. He had enlisted in the Marines in 1942 and two-and-a-half years later had landed on Iwo Jima as a platoon sergeant. Twice hit by machine-gun bullets he refused evacuation from the battlefield. Fisher left that terrible island with a Silver Star Medal and a recommendation for a commission. As a first lieutenant, Fisher had commanded a rifle company in the legendary Chosin Reservoir campaign during the Korean War and had won the Navy Cross Medal there. By the time of Starlite, he was balding and aging but still tough. He was a rough and profane man who suffered no fools. He took care of his men and they loved him. They proudly called themselves "The Magnificent Bastards."

HOTEL SIX

On the evening before Starlite, the officers and NCOs gathered at the Hotel Company, 2/4, command post. 1st Lieutenant Homer K. "Mike" Jenkins, the company commander, was brief. Using the standard five-paragraph format, he told his men that a large enemy force was thought to be south of the Tra Bong River, and he generally outlined his plan of attack and assigned objectives on a map. The 1st Platoon, under Lt Chris Cooney, was to travel with the command group and act as a reserve. Lieutenant Jack Sullivan's 2d Platoon was to secure Hill 43, which the Vietnamese call Pho Thinh Mountain, southwest of the helicopter landing zones. And Lt Bob Morrison was to use his 3d Platoon to attack and secure the village of Nam Yen 3, northeast of the LZ. Hotel Company and the remainder of 2/4 would either drive the enemy toward the sea and 3/3, which was landing over the beach, or they would have the enemy driven toward them. In no case did their experience with the VC indicate that the Viet Cong would stand and fight.

There were a couple of things about this operation that worried Mike Jenkins. One was that 1/7 came in to man the lines so Hotel Company could get plenty of rest. The other was that they there would be naval gunfire on call during the operation. Neither one of these had precedent in their experience in Vietnam.

Jenkins told his men to be saddled up and ready for the pickup at first light. He closed the briefing with instructions to draw plenty of ammunition and fill up all their canteens.

Jenkins was one of the few junior officers in the battalion with combat experience. Months before his Hawaii-based unit went to Vietnam, Jenkins had volunteered for an advisory program that was rotating young officers into Vietnam for sixty to ninety days. But Jenkins was a Marine Corps Reserve officer and Bull Fisher was determined that only Regular officers be sent from his battalion to get combat experience. Jenkins was not a Marine who gave up easily; he kept after his boss to send him to Vietnam. After five or six trips to the colonel's office to repeat his request over a period of some months, Fisher finally shook his head and said, "Pack your bags, you're leaving tomorrow."

In the early days before the commitment of American ground troops in Vietnam, transportation to that country was dicey. Traveling with another officer on the same orders, it took Jenkins a couple of weeks of bouncing around the Far East on space-available flights before he finally made it to Saigon. At the initial briefing the dozen or so visiting officers were told by the colonel in charge of Marine advisors, "Statistically speaking, one of you is going to go home in a box, two of you will be critically wounded, two of you will be walking wounded, and the rest of you will not receive a scratch during your short stay here." The colonel's prophecy was close. Five of the new officers in the briefing went together on an operation with Vietnamese Marines. Two of those went home in boxes and two were critically wounded, but Jenkins emerged from his tour unscathed and with combat experience.

His adventure was to be invaluable on the Starlite battlefield toward which he was headed.

Jenkins expected Hotel Company to make contact with the enemy. The day before the operation he and a couple of other officers were taken on an aerial reconnaissance of the battle area. Jenkins was sitting in the door of a helicopter comparing the terrain with his map, when someone fired a .45-caliber weapon at the aircraft. The fire appeared to come from Landing Zone Blue, Hotel's landing zone for the following day. Jenkins knew it was a .45 when one of the rounds spent its fury on the skin of the chopper and rolled across the deck toward him. He picked it up and put it in his pocket for a souvenir.

Corporal Victor Nunez came away from Jenkins's pre-operation briefing with the understanding that the enemy force would number about two hundred. Not too formidable, Nunez thought, but it was worrisome enough to keep him from getting a sound night's sleep. As Nunez was filling canteens, he chatted a moment with LCpl Joe "J. C." Paul, a fire team leader. Paul finished with, "Vic, take care of yourself tomorrow." "You, too, buddy," was the reply. It was the last time they would meet.

Lance Corporal Ernie Wallace got the word passed along to him second-hand. He knew, though, that he could expect to see some action.

Many of the young Marines were more relaxed about the operation. After all, they had a lot of "long walks in the sun" behind them and knew that usually nothing much happened. Up to this point in the war, encounters between American and VC forces rarely involved more than a platoon of the enemy. The enemy sent his larger forces against the ARVN, not against American firepower and technology. Anticipating a typical operation, few 2/4 Marines carried a whole lot of extra gear or supplies. Most stuffed a couple of C-ration cans into their pockets, reasoning that the Chulai airstrip was only a twenty-minute helicopter ride away and resupply would be routine. Nor did the Marines wear the flak jackets that would later become ubiquitous in the war.

2/4. 0600

Bull Fisher decided to go into LZ White with Echo Company. This would put him physically in the center of his three companies in the field, between Golf Company to the north and Hotel Company to the south. Foxtrot Company was left at Chulai as part of the airfield security.

The Bull had had a new major report for duty. At the time 2/4 had neither an executive officer (XO) nor an operations officer (S-3), which were both assignments for majors. The new man would normally have expected to fill one of these positions in the field. Fisher decided to leave the inexperienced officer in the rear as his liaison and to take GySgt Ed Garr with him to serve as his all-around guy. Garr was a seasoned veteran with combat experience in Korea, a man that the colonel knew well, liked, and trusted.

As Garr thought about his role on the operation, he got little sleep that night, but probably more than if he was still a company gunnery sergeant. Gunnery Sergeant is both a rank *and* a title in the Marine Corps. Shortened to "gunny," the title was that of a rifle company operations chief. The gunny was the man the company commanders counted on to get things done. If Gunny Garr had still been in Hotel Company, his previous assignment, he undoubtedly would have been up all night, getting the troops and supplies ready to go.

Early in the Vietnam War there were a lot of personal and unauthorized weapons floating around. When someone came up with a Browning Automatic Rifle (BAR) the old workhorse from World War II and Korea,[23] Lieutenant Colonel Fisher decided to arm Garr with it, because Fisher liked the weapon and the gunny was one of the few Marines in 2/4 who knew how to operate and clean it. The BAR was no fun to carry, however. With bipod, it weighed about twenty pounds, and a full allotment of magazines could double the load.

After hauling it around for a few weeks Garr managed to trade it, with the colonel's approval, for a Thompson submachine-gun, which he painted green and dubbed the "Green Hornet." The Thompson or "tommygun" spit out a lot of heavy .45-caliber slugs, but it was not particularly accurate. Garr finally managed to trade *that*, the day before Starlite, for a Smith and Wesson .38 Special revolver. He was glad to be unburdened of both the BAR and the tommygun. He was also armed with his standard-issue .45-automatic pistol.

Allowing for temperatures of 110 degrees and a load allowance of 240 pounds per man because of ammunition, weapons, and gear, the helicopters could only carry seven Marines per lift. Flight times and turn-around distances were closely calculated in order to compute fuel loads. A choice had to be made between carrying a light fuel load and more men and equipment, and thus having to refuel more often, or more fuel and fewer men and less equipment.

Landing Hour for the helicopters was set for fifteen minutes later than H-hour on the beach. This would permit concentration of maximum effort in securing the beach and then at the landing zones and thus prevent having to split support resources between the two. Further, it was important that the stronger force, the one landed over the beach with tanks and other heavy equipment, be established first. The helicopters did not have sufficient load capacity for the tanks and other such machinery. Some of the tracked vehicles that were to come ashore with 3/3 were designated to link up with Hotel, 2/4, by mid-morning.

FIRE SUPPORT. 0615

At 0615, fifteen minutes before H-hour on the beach, Kilo Battery, 4/12, which had displaced to firing positions on the northern bank of the Tra Bong in the Chulai tactical area of responsibility on the night of August 17, began 155mm artillery prep fires against the helicopter landing zones. At H-hour, 0630, the 1st Marine Aircraft Wing units Marine Attack squadrons (VMA) 225 and 214, flying A4 Skyhawks; and Marine Fighter/Attack (VMFA) squadrons 311, 513, and 542, flying F4 Phantoms; and Marine Observation Squadron (VMO) 2, with UH-1 Huey gunships, also began to prep the helicopter landing zones with eighteen tons of bombs and napalm. Two U.S. Army aviation platoons and part of a third, which were operating with the ARVN in this area and had become very familiar with it, supported the operation as well.

The 3d Platoon, 1st 8-inch Howitzer Battery (SP) chimed in with its heavy-hitting big guns. At the time of its landing at Chulai the battery's six M-53 weapons were the longest shooters in Vietnam, with a maximum range of nearly twelve miles. Their reach permitted them to support the operation without leaving the Chulai base.

CHAPTER 6

"LAND THE LANDING FORCE!"

As the sky lightened behind them the Marines of 3/3 looked westward past the bows of the ships at the dusky coastline. The sun was not yet over the horizon. In the early morning light the shore appeared so dark as to be almost black but for a narrow strip of silvery surf dividing land from the sea.

The first command came, "All Marines lay up to your debarkations stations." The Marines of Kilo and India companies filed down into the well deck of the USS *Cabildo* and packed themselves into the amtracs with a minimum of confusion.

When Commodore McKinney issued the traditional command, "Land the landing force. Away all boats!" the landing craft splashed into the South China Sea, one at a time, and swam away from the mother ships. The Marines could hear bombs bursting ashore as fixed-wing aircraft prepped the helicopter landing zones.

The hatches in amphibian tractors leak, so when the vehicle Pfc Glenn Johnson was in came down the ramp of the LSD and hit the ocean, water poured in through the rear hatch. The landing ahead was momentarily forgotten as the Marines all shifted forward a bit to keep from getting wet.

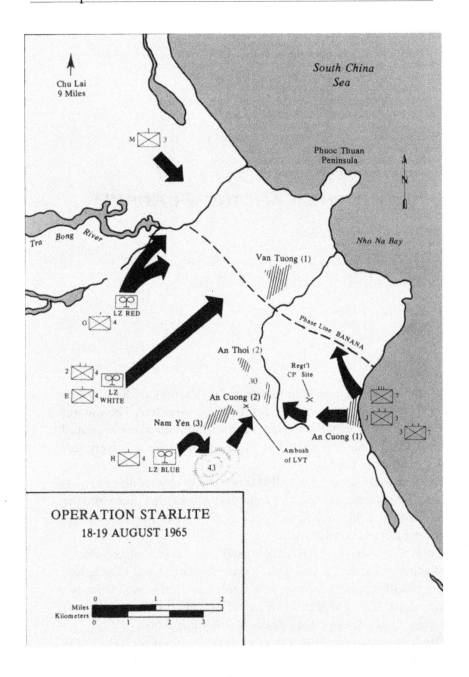

Chu Lai
9 Miles

South China
Sea

M ⊠ 3

Phuoc Thuan
Peninsula

N

Tra Bong River

Nho Na Bay

Van Tuong (1)

LZ RED

G ⊠ 4

Phase Line BANANA

An Thoi (2)

Regt'l
CP Site

2 ⊠ 4
LZ WHITE
E ⊠ 4

30

An Cuong (2)

Nam Yen (3)

III ⊠ 7

J ⊠ 3

3 ⊠ 7

Ambush
of LVT

An Cuong (1)

H ⊠ 4
LZ BLUE

43

OPERATION STARLITE
18-19 AUGUST 1965

0   1   2
Miles
Kilometers
0   1   2   3

Low in the water and coughing clouds of blue exhaust smoke, the tractors circled until they got properly aligned. Captain Bruce Webb's India Company was in the first wave, on the left, and Capt Jay Doub's Kilo Company was on the right.

Once in place, the amtracs moved out together toward the beach, temporarily streaking the sea with wakes of white, foamy water. Most of the troops remained calm during the noisy, cramped ride to the objective. There was no sense of foreboding; they had done this before.

As the amphibian tractors moved steadily toward the shore, a flight of Marine aircraft strafed the beach in front of An Cuong 1, 3/3's first objective. The decision was made at some higher level that the beach area not be bombed, because of the possibility of causing civilian casualties in the village.

The edge of the sun finally burst over the horizon and illuminated the objective area. The heat was already building toward the compression-chamber steambath that sucked up energy and purpose.

The VC opened fire with rifles and automatic weapons. Dutch-born Cpl Jake Germeraad, an 81mm mortar section leader, watched as an amtrac crewman came down out of his hatch for a moment. A Marine who was curious about what was going on moved up into the crewman's seat and stuck his head and shoulders out to take a look. He was immediately shot through the shoulder and fell back into the tractor, spurting blood. The wounded Marine had collected a Purple Heart Medal sometime before under questionable circumstances.

Many Marines were superstitious about Purple Hearts. They thought that if they accepted one they did not truly deserve that they would earn it later by getting hit with a serious wound. This incident did nothing to dispel that philosophy.

As the amtracs neared the beach the Marines went through last-minute mental checklists, conscientiously going over their gear and thinking about their assignments.

Lance Corporal Chris Buchs looked up out of one of the hatches in his tractor at the rising sun. When the vehicle slowed right before it reached the soft sand of the beach and nosed slightly upward, Buchs and the other members of Cpl Robert O'Malley's squad locked and loaded their weapons in preparation for rushing out as soon as the ramp was dropped. They did not know what would greet them.

The beach at An Cuong 1 is a soft, white, sandy shelf less than thirty meters across at most places. It runs north and south and is about a kilometer in length. It is a gentle, white crescent bordered by a dark rocky hill on the north and a stream that flows through black, rocky lowland on the south. Landward, the vegetation lies thick and green around the ancient fishing village. A few hundred meters inland, in most areas, the sand disappears and the soil becomes the familiar laterite that is the color of dried blood. On the morning of the landing, like all mornings, there were several tiny round fishing boats lying with their nets on the sand. The air was hot and still. The temperature was to rise to 95 degrees before noon and would rise to over 105 later in the day.

The amtracs, about thirty of them, came out of the water more or less on line, dropped their ramps on the beach, and disgorged Marines.

A few of the Marines did not have much experience with amtracs. Private First Class Chuck Fink of India Company was one of them. He had been among the first to board his amtrac before it left the mother ship. He thought that the ramp would drop from the rear of the vehicle after it hit the beach. He didn't want to be the first man off the machine on a hostile shore, so he had squeezed his way up to the front of the tractor and faced to the rear. He expected to be the last man off. As his tractor came ashore and gained traction on the sand its bow pointed slightly upwards. The rearward-facing Fink was astonished and dismayed to find that the ramp was *behind* him, that it was beginning to drop, and that he had not only figured wrong about which end it was on, but he had to turn around before he could get off. Just as he recovered from his mistake, took a deep breath, and chased his shadow across the ankle-deep sand an explosion punctuated the activity around him.

From the ground just landward of the beach, grit and debris geysered upward in a noxious cloud of black smoke and flew everywhere. The blast was caused when Duong Hong Minh set off his command-detonated mine. It is likely that all the Marine combat power coming across the water convinced Minh to set it off as soon as he could, so he could clear out. Moreover, his instructions to fall back and protect the regimental command post colored his decision. Fortunately for the Marines, Minh's anxiety attack caused him to detonate the device prematurely. No Marine was killed or wounded, but the blast convinced the skeptical among them that the enemy knew they were there.

INDIA COMPANY, 3/3. 0630

As the smoke and dirt cleared, Pfc Chuck Fink spotted an elderly Vietnamese running away from the beach. The man didn't appear to be armed; indeed, he seemed to be hobbling with a cane. Fink wondered if he should shoot him. He asked himself what John Wayne would do and finally just stood there and watched the man disappear into the brush.

INDIA COMPANY, 3/3. 0645

Following a brief pause in the wake of the explosion on the beach, India Company, 3/3, shifted a bit to the south and proceeded into the brushy area beyond the sand. The company commander, Capt Bruce Webb, sent a squad to check out the source of the explosion. These Marines found a large hole with wires leading to it through a trench and on back into a cave complex. After they confirmed the origin of the blast, and found no enemy there, they commenced movement without incident through the southern half of An Cuong 1, which was adjacent to the beach.

A short way into the wooded area, the action ground to one of those halts that occur in combat while the situation is being reassessed. Private First Class Glenn Johnson and a squad went on a short patrol and discovered a VC hospital; they found bloody bandages and beds up on stilts but no other equipment. They were between one hundred to two hundred meters in from the beach at this point, and isolated from the rest of the unit. They didn't know what to do, so they moved back to report their findings to India Company.

KILO COMPANY

Abreast, and to Webb's right, Capt Jay Doub's Kilo Company came ashore and moved rapidly inland. A few rounds of enemy fire snapped these Marines awake to the fact that this was an opposed landing. Lt Burt Hinson's 1st Platoon secured and searched its portion of An Cuong 1 with little resistance. As it went through the village, Sgt Frank Blank, Hinson's 1st Squad leader, reported seeing several VC as they ran from the huts away from the Marines. Hinson personally saw one or two dead VC on the ground.

Doub's 2d and 3d platoons moved through the village and secured the high ground to the west, paused for a bit to check their orientation, and then moved inland around three-hundred meters.

3/3 COMMAND GROUP

The 3/3 battalion command group, embarked in flat-bottomed landing craft, followed behind the assault waves. The landing was conducted smoothly except that the landing craft carrying the 3/3 Alpha command group, including LtCol Joe Muir, became stuck for about twenty minutes on a submerged sand bar about four hundred meters off the beach. Landing an hour after low tide had a price, but this was one paid in inconvenience, not in blood.

KILO, 3/3. 0645

Lieutenant Burt Hinson kept his men going until they came up to the crest of Hill 22, a small rise to the west and a bit north of the landing area. Lieutenant Jack Kelly's platoon was tied in on the extreme right flank of India Company, and Hinson's 1st Squad, commanded by Sgt Frank Blank, was tied in to Kelly.

Hinson never got a chance to walk the line and see where it was tied in. While the Marines from Kilo Company were resting and planning their next activity a great deal of action started in the India sector, to their left.

Just before activity with India Company intensified, two or three amtracs, including a command tractor with 3/3's LtCol Joe Muir aboard, somehow got out ahead of Kilo. When Captain Doub asked for a position report from the battalion command group, he checked his map and found that Muir's group was in front of Kilo Company. Doub radioed Muir, "Colonel, what are you doing out in front of me? Are you trying to tell me that the CP group is now five hundred meters out in front of the lead company?" The amused Muir ordered Kilo forward to its next objective, and to be quick about it.

After just a few yards, the 2d and 3d platoons of Kilo Company attracted a tremendous amount of automatic weapons fire from across their front, and halted in place. Much of the fire came from another piece of high ground to the right front, and some from a trenchline to the left. This fire came from a delaying force commanded by Phan Tan Huan, who had the mission of screening the relocation of the regimental command post.

Lieutenant Hinson did not know that one of his casualties was Sgt Frank Blank, his 1st Squad leader, who was hit in the stomach and died. At about the same time Hinson's platoon sergeant, SSgt "Catfish" Campbell, took a single round in his scrotum. He was medevaced later in the day, stitched up, and returned to the fight that night.

Unbeknownst to either Kilo Company, or the 3/3 CP group, Jay Doub's Marines were headed directly for the 1st VC Regiment command post, which was located in the village of Van Tuong 1. The fire that greeted Kilo Company was designed to buy time and permit the withdrawal of the CP to Van Tuong 3, farther to the west, if necessary. Duong Hong Minh, who had set off the initial charge at the beach, and Huan were in charge of the force that faced Doub's Marines. Nguyen Dinh Trong, the political officer who had inherited command of the regiment in the absence of his commander, ordered his men to pack up and prepare to move if it became necessary.

Except for one squad in Burt Hinson's 1st Platoon, Kilo Company was pinned down by VC fire. Hinson grabbed this squad of Marines and took off after the enemy. He shouted encouragement to his men and fired his .45 at the VC as he moved. The meager force fought its way up a slope to the southeast of the village of An Thoi, about a kilometer from An Cuong 2. By driving the enemy and their automatic weapons from the crest of the slope, Hinson and his squad relieved the pressure along the entire 3/3 front. To this day he has no idea how many Viet Cong his Marines killed. He just remembers blazing away at the enemy on his way up the hill.

Upon reaching the crest Hinson saw four VC running down a path and squeezed the trigger of an empty .45-caliber pistol he had pointed at them. He was completely out of ammunition despite the fact he had gotten all those extra rounds and magazines from Staff Sergeant Bradley.

With the VC along this sector on the run, 3/3 began moving forward again. It was here that Burt Hinson was told of Sergeant Blank's death and that Staff Sergeant Campbell had been wounded. Jay

Doub later remarked to Lt Dave Steel, the battalion assistant operations officer, that he didn't have any idea why Hinson was alive, because every type of weaponry the enemy possessed was fired at him as he led his people forward. Doub, "The Boiled Owl," was not a person who normally got excited by something like this. Burt Hinson was awarded the Silver Star Medal for his heroic actions this day.

At the same time Hinson's action was taking place, the reserve 1st Platoon passed through the line, assaulted, and carried the trenchline to the left. Because of the action in the adjacent sectors, Kilo Company was not able to advance any further that day, so it dug in about a kilometer short of the 1st VC Regiment command post. Huan and Minh had accomplished their mission; they had delayed the Marine advance on their command group.

LIMA, 3/3. 0730

Captain Jim McDavid's Lima Company, the battalion reserve, and the second wave of the assault, came ashore next. That wave also included the battalion secondary, or "Bravo" command group, with Maj Andy Comer in charge. The Bravo command group vessel, an LCM-8, struck a submerged bar at high-speed, causing numerous minor injuries to those embarked because of the sudden impact. The boat was able to retract rapidly and deposited Comer's group on dry land a little after 0730.

Lieutenant David Steel, the assistant operations officer, landed with Major Comer's Bravo command group just as a VC machine gun low on the right of the beach opened fire. A redheaded lance corporal was talking with Steel on the beach and the lieutenant cautioned him to be careful. Within seconds the lance corporal was hit in the chest and slightly wounded. Marines quickly silenced the gun, and there was little additional fire from that sector.

THE RLT HQ COMES ASHORE

Shortly after 0730 and closely following the 3/3 command groups, the tactical control elements of the RLT-7 headquarters landed on Green Beech. By noon, when the RLT-7 command post was established a thousand meters inland, overall command of the operation shifted from Comdr William McKinney, the amphibious squadron commander, to Col Peat Peatross, the landing force commander.

Peatross could have gone in with the heliborne force, but, in accordance with doctrine, he chose to travel with the amphibious force. This permitted him to employ his command amphibian tractor's communications capabilities and to be closest to the heavy elements of his command and his logistics base. In other words, he was best able from that location to control the battle. His command, control, and logistics organization was set up and functioning by the end of the day.

CHAPTER 7

ASSAULT FROM THE AIR

While the Marines of 3/3 were crossing the beach, BLT 2/4 was staged for pickup. The number of helicopters that came for them was amazing to the Marines. Most of them had never seen so many in one place before. They kept coming in, one after the other.

Major Homer Jones, a former helicopter pilot and now fighter jock, approached Maj Al Bloom, the HMM-361 operations officer. Jones was an old friend of Bloom's and wanted to know if he could go along as co-pilot. Bloom quickly assented. On their way from the ready room to the aircraft, MSgt R. M. Hooven, the maintenance chief, intercepted Bloom. Hooven wanted to fly as crew chief and, moreover, he wanted to bring along 1st Sergeant Dorsett as gunner. Dorsett, an old infantry type, had just joined the squadron and was less than impressed with what he regarded as the unmilitary appearance and attitude of "Airedales," a pejorative that ground troops used to describe aviation Marines. Master Sergeant Hooven wanted to show the first sergeant what his Marines could do. Major Bloom agreed and loaded up his high-priced and over-qualified crew, lifted off, and followed Lieutenant Colonel Childers's lead in the fifty-minute flight to the pick-up area.

Golf Company was loaded first to make the run into Landing Zone Red. The company landed on the zone without incident beginning at 0645. The troops were all on the ground by 0715 and headed toward their first objective to the northeast.

Echo Company boarded next and took off for Landing Zone White. The company quickly disembarked and set up a perimeter to await the battalion command group, which was to land directly after it.

2/4. 0700

Lieutenant Colonel Bull Fisher; GySgt Ed Garr; Captain Riley, the assistant operations officer (S-3A); and the colonel's radio operators were on one helo team, and all boarded together. In his months in Vietnam, Garr learned to check the deck of a chopper for spent cartridges to see if the door gunners had fired their weapons. If they had, it was a sure sign that they had been into a hot landing zone. All Marines dreaded going into a hot LZ. There is no more helpless feeling than dropping into an LZ under fire and having bullets pop up through the floor of one's helicopter. This time there were no spent cartridges, and the crew chief had no news about what was happening on the ground. Garr was greatly relieved.

Fisher's command group flew to LZ White and, after it landed, followed Echo Company in the direction of its first objective, to the northeast. The VC, who manned firing positions on a ridgeline east and northeast of the LZ, engaged Echo Company with a moderate amount of mortar, automatic weapons, and small arms fire.

The last company to board was Mike Jenkins's Hotel. Pfc Jim Scott, Lieutenant Jenkins's company radio operator, and Pfc Morris Robinson, Jenkins's battalion radio operator, piled aboard with their skipper. Scott looked out to see Pfc Henry Jordan run by to get on his chopper. Jordan had a smile on his face, and his thumb was pointed up. The day before the operation, he had received a bunch of pictures of a family reunion from home. Jordan was a happy Marine.

Back in LZ White, the call came over the radio for Sudden Death 6, Bull Fisher's radio call sign, to remain in the LZ because Colonel Peatross was coming in and wanted to talk to him.

While it waited, the battalion command group had visual contact with Echo Company, which was still engaged and taking casualties.

They could see Marines under small arms and mortar fire going up the hill. Echo was a fine company, not one to back down from anything, so the troops doggedly kept at the enemy.

Some of the helicopters had already made multiple trips, so those lowest on fuel peeled off for a refueling stop prior to picking up their last load, which was Hotel Company, bound for Landing Zone Blue.

INTO A HOT LZ

Private First Class Dick Boggia was a Marine with a big job. He was an eighteen-year-old who had never had an eighteenth birthday. He had crossed the Pacific by ship, and when they passed the International Dateline the calendar had jumped a day ahead and skipped the anniversary of his birth. Boggia was the junior man in his machine-gun squad, an ammo humper who was burdened with 400 rounds of the heavy 7.62mm ammunition for the M60 machine-gun. Inasmuch as the squad was shorthanded, he also had to carry the tripod and the traversing and elevating (T&E) mechanism for the gun. This was in addition to his rifle, ammunition, and personal gear. Despite the enormous load Boggia was proud and excited to be going on the operation. He had been told that Hotel, 2/4's mission would be to force the VC into a blocking position set up by other Marines. This was one of the few times Boggia had ridden in a helicopter and he enjoyed the ride. By chance, he drew the seat opposite the door gunner, so he could look out the door at the countryside. He was amazed at how beautiful it was as the mist burned off and revealed the greenery below. As they got closer to the objective, he could see helicopter gunships strafing nearby hills.

Corporal Dick "Nootch" Tonucci was an infantry squad leader with Lt Jack Sullivan's 2d Platoon. On the way into the landing zone he worried about getting linked up with the others and finding some cover while forming a 360-degree perimeter around the LZ to protect the subsequent waves that landed. He did not think it would be a routine landing; he was ready for the worst. It would not have comforted him if he had known in advance that the landing zone they selected was, by pure chance, within the defense perimeter of the 60th VC Battalion. He had been told the LZ would not be hot, but his blood ran cold on the approach to the landing zone. He could not stand helicopters.

Corporal Ernie Wallace was Corporal Tonucci's machine-gunner. Wallace's ammo humper, Pfc Jim Kehres, was not even supposed to be there. He was only seventeen years old, and while the Marine Corps permitted the enlistment of seventeen-year-olds, regulations forbade sending them into a combat zone until they were eighteen. Somehow Kehres had gotten by the administrators.

Machine-gun squad leader Juan Moreno knew that they were going to make contact with the enemy, but he tried not to think about dying, because he was afraid it would keep him from concentrating on what he must do. He worried about his men and thought that they were a great bunch of happy-go-lucky kids. Once a fight started they immediately turned into men. But after it was over he had to get on top of them again: "Clean your weapon, brush your teeth, take your malaria pill . . ."

Tonucci's bird was one of the first to touch down, and the Marines all jumped off. As team leader, Tonucci was first out. He directed the men to their spots on the LZ. Jimmy Brooks the tall, thin lance corporal they called "Buzzard" was off, Lou Grant was off, and a couple of other guys.

They were just getting oriented and setting up around the landing zone when enemy fire tore into them from Hill 43, to the southwest. The Army Huey gunships from the 7th Airlift Platoon took the VC on the hill under fire as the Marines completed their defensive perimeter around the landing zone. Three VC were killed at this position as the Marines struggled to attain fire superiority. When one of the Army pilots, Maj Don Radcliff, was shot through the neck and killed and another crew member was wounded supporting the Marines on LZ Blue, his section of aircraft withdrew. The major was part of a site selection team looking for a camp for the 1st Cavalry Division, just then en route to Vietnam. He had volunteered for the mission and had become his division's first KIA in Vietnam. The 1st Cavalry Division named its first base Camp Radcliff in Vietnam in his honor.

Tonucci had just started moving his squad toward a dike, which would provide some cover, when LCpl Jimmy Brooks appeared to trip. "Nootch, I'm hit. I'm hit in the shoulder." Tonucci carried Brooks to the dike and, while he was ripping the Marine's shirt open, noted that there was blood all over the place. Where was it coming from? Then he saw that Brooks shoulder wound was merely the entry point for a .50-caliber round that had gone all the way through the young man. A .50-caliber projectile, a, half-inch across and two inches long, packs a very lethal punch. Tonucci cradled Brooks in his arms as the corpsman gave Brooks a shot of morphine. The mortally wounded Marine turned blue and his life passed out of him. Brooks was the first man Nootch had ever seen die. He would not be the last.

The helicopters kept coming in, adding the roar of their engines, the clattering of their blades, and the smell of exhaust to the hammering of gunfire and the stench of cordite and blood. The VC fire mounted as the remainder of the company landed. When a mortar round detonated near Tonucci's position the young corporal got on the radio and passed the word to get some elevation on the mortars, that they were coming up short and endangering friendly troops. He quickly found out that they were not friendly mortars. Lieutenant Mike Jenkins heard the same explosion and yelled to one of his radio operators, "Find out what the hell they are doing over there. Who threw that damn grenade?" Jenkins, too, quickly found out that the explosion was an enemy mortar round.

Other Marines died in the first few minutes of the operation. One was Henry Jordan, who had happily boarded his helicopter, pictures of his family in his pocket.

As one of the last few waves came into LZ Blue under fire, SSgt Coy Overstreet, a helicopter crew chief, spotted khaki-clad man with a weapon racing toward his bird on the LZ. He figured it was a friendly interpreter until a black-pajama-wearing man jumped up and joined the man in khaki. It was the first time Overstreet had ever seen the enemy run *toward* a Marine helicopter. He swung his M60 machine-gun around to bear on the two and prepared to fire when the pair passed a dike. As they did, what Overstreet had thought were about twenty small bushes jumped up and also ran toward the LZ. They were well-camouflaged enemy soldiers in echelon formation, firing their weapons right at him. The Marine opened up, nailed the original two, and caused havoc among the others. As his helicopter began to lift off it was severely jolted when what appeared to be an anti-armor weapon detonated immediately beneath it. The pilot poured on full power and got out of the LZ as quickly as possible. Once he got the helicopter in the air and stabilized, he came up on the company radio net and told Jim Scott, Mike Jenkins's radio operator, that the Marines were surrounded by Viet Cong, who were disguised as bushes and could be detected from the air.

The .50-caliber machine gun that got Jimmy Brooks was directly in front of Hotel Company, on Hill 43, and it and some snipers were able to pin down the Marines. Like most of the others, Cpl Victor Nunez was firing back at the Viet Cong, but the enemy was well camouflaged, very hard to see. Only the fact that their positions were so close to the LZ allowed Nunez to pick out the brief yellow-blue muzzle flashes on which to train his machine gun.

The Marines were taking a lot of fire from a nearby hootch. A 3.5-inch rocket team fired a round at it but missed. Lieutenant Sullivan grabbed the rocket tube from the gunner, had a round loaded, and fired the weapon himself. His aim was off; the rocket hit the ground just in front of the target. Luckily it took a perfect bounce off the ground and flew into the hootch, where it detonated.

The VC got the range of the helicopters that were bringing the last of Hotel Company into the LZ. One Marine had his jaw shot off, and one of the choppers took hits from five or six rounds of automatic weapons fire. A pilot, Capt Howard Henry, noted that the Marines just shut their eyes and dropped to the ground in order to ignore the fire.

Shrapnel wounded 1stLt Ramsey Myatt, a co-pilot with HMM-361, as he flew a medevac mission. He bandaged the wound and continued to fly. The enemy gunfire damaged a rotor blade, which Myatt's crew chief, SSgt Dale Bredeson, changed in about ten minutes. Later that morning Myatt took a bullet in the leg, but he refused to leave the controls and kept flying until he became too weak to continue. The enemy fire seriously damaged the aircraft, so it limped back to base, where it was grounded for the rest of the battle.

Another pilot, Stu Kendall, was shot through the leg and right hand. His co-pilot took over and got the aircraft to a safe area.

No flight crewmember becomes accustomed to bullets popping through the skin of his ship, but on this day it became commonplace. To the airmen it sounded like being in the butts of the rifle range.

After one of the early medevacs, Maj Al Bloom was lifting off and gaining speed when he spotted a row of prone VC, lined up shoulder-to-shoulder to his left and firing at the Marine infantry to his front. 1st Sergeant Dorsett, the infantryman-turned-door-gunner, knew what to do. Because of the relative position to the target Dorsett was in perfect enfilade alignment. He got off a long burst that raked the entire enemy line. Bloom was not sure how many hits were made, because he decided it would be a bad idea to circle back for a body count. The VC had not seen them coming but undoubtedly would be looking for them if they made a second pass.

As planned, the 2d Platoon of Hotel Company began its attack against Hill 43, and the 3d Platoon moved to attack Nam Yen 3. Lieutenant Jenkins traveled with the 1st Platoon, his reserve, and moved off in the direction of Nam Yen 3, which was his company's main objective.

The Viet Cong who occupied both objectives stood and fought. Both assaulting platoons ran into stiffer opposition than anticipated, and both attacks stalled.

Lieutenant Sullivan's 2d Platoon, which tried to take Hill 43, got no further than the bottom of the hill.

Alert for the enemy, LCpl Ernie Wallace spotted a large number of Viet Cong moving down a trenchline toward the Marines' rear. He came upon them in a storm of machine-gun fire, rushing them as he fired his gun from the hip and from the shoulder. The big gunner was good at his trade. He single-handedly killed an estimated twenty-five VC.

In the confusion, Wallace became separated from his ammo humper Pfc Jim Kehres. Unsure about what to do, Kehres helped out wherever he thought he was needed and was later awarded a Navy Commendation Medal for evacuation of casualties under fire.

Mike Jenkins halted the attack and requested additional air strikes against Hill 43. F4 Phantoms from VMFA-513 and VMFA-342 pounded the hill with high-explosive bombs and napalm. When the Marines were lucky they got Snake Eye bombs, which were particularly effective when used with napalm in a "snake-and-nape" attack. The napalm would drive the enemy into the open and render them vulnerable to the fragmentation bombs that quickly followed. The Snake Eye bomb was especially developed for close air support. When Snake Eyes are released from an airplane, their large fins open to make a distinctive "pop" and slow the descent to the ground. This gives the plane time to get away and avoid being hit by the fragments of their own bombs. If you were a Marine on the ground, and close enough to hear the fins pop open, you were getting *close* air support indeed. Napalm is simply gasoline mixed with a thickener that jells the fuel. It not only burns with the heat and intensity of gasoline, it sticks to its targets. It creates a fiery hell and is a terrifying weapon.

While his 2d Platoon was struggling with Hill 43, Lt Mike Jenkins and his other two platoons formed up and moved toward Nam Yen 3. They started a slow winding trek down a long ravine into a series of tree lines surrounded by rock- hard, dried-up rice paddies covered with stubble. There were still helicopter gunships available, and fixed-wing Skyhawks and Phantoms that bombed and strafed everything that looked like a target. Black smoke billowed out of the ground and tree lines hit by previous fire missions. While skirting a large dried-up rice paddy by following the surrounding tree line the Marines took some sporadic sniper fire. Despite the danger, Pfc Dick Boggia, who was moving with his machine-gun team leader, Corporal Renfro, and with LCpl Ken Stankiewicz, the gunner, felt fairly secure. After all, his fellow Marines were all around him. Sergeant Jerry Tharp, inspired confidence and stood out among the NCOs by walking around upright, ignoring the sniper rounds that were snapping about.

THE ATTACK ON NAM YEN 3

As Hotel, 2/4's 1st and 3d platoons closed on Nam Yen 3 the first sign of life from the village was a black-pajama-clad man who emerged from nowhere and ran along the edge of the little settlement. Several Marines shot at him as he disappeared into some high grass, apparently unscathed. It may have been the man's purpose to encourage a number of Marines to follow him into an ambush. The Marines were to learn the hard way that this was a favored enemy tactic. One or two of the enemy would leap up and run through a killing zone well covered by other Viet Cong. Pursuing Marines would be trapped as they crossed the zone. In this case the Marines from Hotel Company only pursued by fire.

Mike Jenkins ordered the 1st Platoon to assault the village and the 3d Platoon to provide a base of fire. Nam Yen 3 remained quiet. No one was shooting at the Marines from the village, but as they drew closer they found camouflaged punji pits and other signs of defensive preparation.

This all changed in a split-second. Fire suddenly poured into Jenkins's men. Without warning plants came to life. Every place the Marines looked there were dozens of bushes moving in all directions. The situation became very, very intense. The VC shot at the Marines from spider holes, hootches, and bunkers. The Marines countered with gunfire and grenades. Snipers tied to trees fired at the Marines from twenty feet in the air.

The 1st Platoon moved past the edge of the village as the VC small arms fire sharpened. Many of the houses in the village doubled as bunkers. When the action started, the sides of the houses dropped down to enable the occupants access to their pre-planned fields of fire. The village was also pitted with cleverly camouflaged one-man spider holes.

The 3d Company, 60th Viet Cong Battalion, commanded by political commissar Nguyen Ngoc Nhuan, occupied the village. The VC's practice of digging in paid off; they were very well organized for a defensive battle.

Jenkins's 3d Platoon and the company command group moved toward Nam Yen 3. There was an open field between them and the village until they ran into a perpendicular stretch of semi-wooded terrain. The point men started toward the village as other Marines hugged the tree line, waiting to advance. The VC let the point get almost on top of them before dropping Pfc Harry Kaus and LCpl Eddie Landry in a fury of automatic weapons fire. Lieutenant Bob Morrison put his platoon into the assault, and his Marines savagely went after the occupied hedgerow, firing as fast as they could from the hip.

Without really realizing what was happening Pfc Dick Boggia found that his platoon was in the assault. He was alongside his gunner, Ken Stankiewicz, as they got down in position to set up their M60 and cover the advance when their section leader Corporal "Rat" Renfro, was hit by enemy fire just a few feet away. Renfro was lying on the ground with his pack spewing fire and smoke from flares he was carrying. Everything was happening too quickly. Stankiewicz turned the M60 over to Boggia and tried to pull Renfro's pack off. The incoming fire was very intense, and seeing what was happening with Renfro terrified Boggia, but he hung in there and got the gun operating against the enemy. Renfro's pack began to burn even more fiercely.

Boggia knew there was other ordnance in the pack, and he expected an explosion momentarily. The unfazed Stankiewicz ignored the danger and finally separated Renfro from his pack. Renfro was then dragged away and medevaced. Boggia never knew what became of him.

The VC gunfire increased, and grenade after grenade exploded among the Marines. The Marines, too, turned up the volume of rifle fire, and reinforced it with machine guns and 3.5-inch rocket launchers. When they got up to the hedgerow they could see large, ghastly piles of enemy bodies. But they could not see into the village itself and could not staunch the torrent of enemy fire. They could get any further into Nam Yen 3.

The rounds seemed to be coming from everywhere, cracking overhead and tearing up the ground around them. The intensity of the fire forced the Marines to withdraw back to the tree line to regroup. Boggia passed the bodies of the two Marines who had been covered with ponchos.

The fire was confusing, particularly so to the young Marines for whom this was the first taste of combat. Grenades seemed to be going off everywhere, there were casualties on both sides; and the smoke, noise, and smells of combat caused a lot of bewilderment.

In the face of overwhelming fire, the 1st Platoon was pulled back out of the village. Mike Jenkins finally reached Lieutenant Colonel Fisher, back at LZ White, and admitted that he had his hands full. This report went back to the RLT headquarters at about the same time Capt Bruce Webb, the commander of India Company, 3/3, reported fire from An Cuong 2, which was out of his area of responsibility but between himself and Jenkins's Hotel Company, 2/4. Webb requested permission to cross over his boundary to attack An Cuong 2 in the hope India could take some of the pressure off Hotel Company. Permission was readily granted.

Mike Jenkins came upon Lt Chris Cooney and told him to get his 1st Platoon back away from Nam Yen, because he was calling more air strikes. The Hotel Company Marines had no sooner moved back toward the paddy area than the aircraft came in and pounded the village with snake and nape. The aviators laid their 250-pound bombs dangerously close to the Marines on the ground. Although the friendly lines were marked with yellow smoke, fragments from one bomb cut down a small tree right next to Jenkins. A hot, sharp, high-velocity fragment of that type will cut a human body in half. The Marines continued to receive small arms fire from the village as the air strike continued.

Fragments from the bombs also made their way over near An Cuong 2, where India Company, 3/3, was attempting to advance to the aid of Hotel Company, 2/4. They wounded several India Company Marines. Jenkins's men saw several human torches—VC covered with jellied gasoline from the napalm run out of the village. The Marines shot them down.

Inasmuch as Hotel, 2/4, was catching fire from all directions, Lieutenant Jenkins decided to handle just one objective at a time and opted to secure Hill 43 first. The hill was the highest piece of terrain within range of small arms, and it was still bedeviling his rear.

Hotel Company recrossed the 500 meters that separated the objectives and, as soon as the air strikes were complete, renewed the attack on the hill. This time Jenkins threw all three of his platoons against the hill.

The Marines encountered heavy fire and had initial problems securing the crest of the hill. The VC fought back tenaciously, but the Marines fought forward just as hard. A timely reinforcement by tanks that had landed over the beach and more Marine air support helped carry the hill.

As the final air strike was conducted Hotel Company evacuated eleven of its own wounded and one KIA. While loading a wounded Marine on a tank Pfc Jim Kehres, who had been helping with with wounded since becoming separated from his gunner, Ernie Wallace, was shot through both buttocks and knocked to the ground. He was himself evacuated.

WITH SUDDEN DEATH SIX

The radios with the 2/4 battalion command group were very busy. They reported that Golf Company was moving to its assigned objective from LZ Red with relatively little contact, that Echo Company had a handle on what was confronting it, and that Hotel Company had stepped in it. Lieutenant Colonel Fisher learned that Hotel had been taken under fire immediately and had problems, but poor radio communications prevented him from getting a clear picture of what was going on.

Waiting in the LZ for Colonel Peatross seemed like an eternity, especially because Fisher's command group was under fire from small arms and the occasional 60mm mortar round.

Peatross flew in, and he and the Bull talked. They were extremely concerned with what was happening to Hotel Company. Although Hotel was just over the next short ridgeline there was no way they could find out what was going on. They knew that 1stLt Mike Jenkins was in a major fight, but the Bull trusted him and was doing what he could to make sure that all the supporting arms knew the priority was for Hotel

Company. After hearing that, Peatross flew back to the regimental CP and Fisher and his group went up the hill behind Echo Company.

In the original attack on the first hill, Echo Company had suffered two KIA and three WIA while three fleeing VC had fallen to a direct hit from a 3.5-inch rocket launcher. As Echo's attack continued the Marines sustained another twelve WIA. It was a constant fight over ground that reminded Gunny Garr of the hill country in Texas, but with hedgerows.

Garr, Captain Riley, Bull Fisher, and the radio operators walked abreast, fairly well spread out. A mortar round landed in front of them and Riley was the only one to get hit. He was able to run to a ditch about twenty yards away along with the Bull and the radio operators. Garr hit the deck and stayed there for a moment. Then, remembering from Korea that two rounds never land in the same place, he crawled over to where the last one had impacted and lay there. The ground was extremely hot, but Garr stayed there for a bit, although the Bull was hollering, "Gunny! Gunny! Are you okay?"

A squad of MPs from the 7th Marines CP was along to act as prisoner security. A Marine from this squad was behind Gunny Garr. Garr asked him if he was okay. He said that, yes, he was, but he sounded a bit uncertain. Garr said, "Crawl over to where I am and we'll wait this out." The Marine, glad of the company, joined him. Colonel Fisher was still yelling; he wanted to know if Garr was okay. Garr yelled back that he was and that he was going to stay in the little depression in the ground with the MP.

Bull and his command group couldn't move, and Echo was temporarily halted by fire. When the VC fire subsided a bit, Garr told the MP, "You follow me and we'll jump into this little ravine." They got over to where the Bull was. Everyone was glad to see Garr because they thought he had been badly hit.

Mortar rounds started impacting along the little gully in which the command group had gone to ground. In addition to Riley there were soon four other wounded in the command group. A staff sergeant who was the acting S-4 for the operation was among them. There was no personnel officer (S-1) on the operation, no sergeant major, and no XO. Now, that Riley was hit, there was no S-3, other than the supporting-arms officers, and there was no staff other than Garr. Bull Fisher looked at Ed Garr and said, "Now, my good gunnery sergeant, you are my S-3 officer." The colonel often prepped his remarks with his officers or staff NCOs with "Now my good lieutenant," or captain, or whatever. It was a sign that the Bull was thinking hard about you.

India Company Leaves Its Zone. 0900

Captain Bruce Webb's India Company, 3/3, had come ashore using a streambed to mark its left flank. The stream ran inland for about 1,800 meters before bending to the north and running parallel to the beach. By about 0900 India had covered the ground to the curve in the streambed and had wheeled around toward the north. Just beyond the stream, and outside India's area of responsibility, was An Cuong 2, now on the India Company left flank.

Within minutes, Captain Webb's Marines spotted a group of about fifteen VC, and then a second group, numbering about twenty, in the center of the village. The VC opened up with small arms and automatic weapons. Webb had an immediate need to protect his flank, so he requested permission to cross over into the 2/4 sector and go after the Viet Cong who were firing at his company. By this time news was coming into the regimental headquarters about Hotel, 2/4's dilemma, so permission was quickly granted. An Cuong 2 lay between India Company and Hotel Company, and Colonel Peatross thought Webb's Marines might be able to relieve the pressure on Hotel as well as guard their own flank.

Permission received, the India Company Marines all took off at high port, running as hard as they could toward the enemy. Downhill and across a flat they went, until they came under fire from a line of small trees. Their attack so surprised the defenders that they overran them and took several prisoners. One of the captured VC, either frightened or unwilling to cooperate with his captors, lay stiff as a board and bit his tongue so badly that blood ran out of his mouth. When 1stSgt Art Petty began evacuating prisoners, he had one of the bigger Marines pick the man up and carry him to a helicopter, so he could be interrogated in the rear. The VC remained in a nearly catatonic state as the aircraft lifted off of the ground.

India Company Marines were busily trying to kill the VC troops they were not able to capture. Lieutenant Richard Purnell, the company XO, spotted a number of VC trying to go around the flank and escape from the Marines down the riverbed. He was attempting to stop them, blazing away with his .45 as fast as he could, yelling, "Get them!"

First Sergeant Petty stood with Captain Webb and watched one of the India Company platoons start across the riverbed. There was a sloping hill on the other bank that was covered with knee-high brush. The two Marines had a grandstand seat as a number of Viet Cong broke and run. Hunters who have seen quail would be familiar with the scene. One VC left his position, ran over to another VC, and stopped for a split second. Then both VC ran over to the next position, and so on until a small group of them was fleeing into the brush together. This may be because the VC broke their forces down into three-man fire teams, that were trained to move together. The Marines cut them down in bunches as they fled.

First Sergeant Petty joined a group to the left of the advance CP group. As they crossed over the riverbed, he heard what he believed were mortar rounds coming in. He hit the deck until the explosions stopped.

The streambed to the company's front ran parallel to the beach. Perpendicular to that was a trenchline or drainage ditch, which ran east and west. Captain Webb's lead elements had crossed to the other side of the trench and a lot of fighting was going on.

The India command group halted briefly before the riverbed and pretty much stretched out on line. One of the nearby Marines took a bullet on the inside of his upper left thigh. The man was screaming and hollering because he thought he had lost his genitals. A corpsman struggled to get the man's pants down and discovered that he had a serious gunshot wound to the thigh but that his manhood was intact. Captain Webb called in a medevac and sent Pfc Glenn Johnson back to get the other evacuees, thinking that they could move up more easily than this Marine could move back. Johnson who stripped off his pack and the satchel charge he was carrying and became the target of the day the instant he got up and started running. Bullets hit all around his feet. He dove into the brushy area to the rear and told the other casualties and those helping them to move up.

One of the Marines hit was Sergeant Massey, the 1st Platoon guide. The bullet glanced off a shovel and went through the fleshy part of Massey's upper arm. Massey decided to stay in the field. He fought through the day and survived Starlite.

THE 2/4 COMMAND GROUP 0900

The 2/4 command group called for a medevac for Captain Riley and the other wounded. As it was inbound, Gunny Garr got on the radio and told the pilot that they were still receiving incoming mortars, then he popped a green smoke grenade in the area where the mortar rounds were landing in order to mark the zone. The pilot brought in his aircraft without hesitation. As the ground troops were loading the casualties Garr noted empty shell casings rolling around on the chopper's deck. It was clear that this bird had already seen some action this day.

ECHO COMPANY, 2/4

Echo Company, 2/4, was getting too far ahead of the command group, which was burdened with a section of two 81mm mortars and several .50-caliber machine guns. Despite the load, they picked up the pace. They also had along a number of Vietnamese Popular Forces troops from the Binh Son District who had been attached to the operation at the last minute.

Echo continued its move to the northeast. At one juncture the Marines spotted about a hundred of the enemy in the open and asked for an artillery fire mission. The Viet Cong were running at a fast trot in the opposite direction, but parallel to the Marines, at a distance of a few hundred yards. They were dressed in dark blue uniforms; carrying weapons, including mortars; and making a strange noise. It sounded to Gunny Garr as if they were grunting.

The Echo Company Marines quickly looked for a way to bring fire to bear on them. They were too distant for effective fire from small arms, and there was a deep ravine between the two forces, which prevented a direct attack. The radio traffic was so thick on the nets that they could not get through using ordinary procedures. Finally they used flash precedence, the designation reserved for extremely important messages, to get through. In this manner they called an artillery fire mission.

The 107mm howtars from 3/12, helilifted into the position occupied by Mike Company, 3/3, poured overwhelming fire into the enemy ranks. Lieutenant Colonel Fisher, who later flew over the impact area in a helicopter, estimated that the howtar mission accounted for ninety enemy dead.

The artillery took the starch out of the enemy resistance and Echo Company was able to continue its push against only minimal opposition.

O'MALLEY'S SQUAD

A section of M48 tanks that had landed in the second wave caught up with India Company, 3/3, just as it was approaching An Cuong 2. Captain Webb assigned Cpl Robert O'Malley's 1st Squad of the 1st Platoon to the tanks.

As the company pushed on and neared the outskirts of the village, enemy fire stiffened and the Marines quickly deployed in assault formation, with the 1st Platoon on the left, the 2d Platoon on the right, and the 3d Platoon was in reserve.

South of the village was a trench about ten feet across and six or seven feet deep. It appeared to be very old, not built especially to be a tank trap, but it was too wide for the tanks to cross, so they were sent along the edge of the trench to the west. The lieutenant in charge of the tanks was aggressive; he led his vehicles, with O'Malley's men on board, away from the main body of India Company. While India Company assaulted into the village to the north, the tanks continued along the trenchline to the west.

Corporal O'Malley had split his squad into three groups. O'Malley, LCpl Chris Buchs, and Pfc Robert Rimpson, rode the first tank; Cpl Forrest Hayden, LCpl James Aaron, and LCpl Merlin Marquardt were in the middle; and the remainder of the squad brought up the rear.

Casualties began to mount elsewhere in the company, but at this point O'Malley's men were not getting enough fire to worry about. They heard a large volume of shooting flare up in the India Company sector and could hear Hotel, 2/4's fire fight in the distance.

The two lead tanks moved out a little faster while the third tank hung back a little as rear security. As they drove around a large hedgerow that gave them some minimal concealment to their right, three BAR rounds suddenly came out of the foliage and stitched Marquardt. O'Malley quickly stopped the tanks and yelled for Hayden and Aaron to get Marquardt off the tank and administer first aid. Then he sent Chris Buchs off to find a corpsman as he and the rest of his squad poured suppressing fire into the hedgerow and worked on Marquardt.

Buchs raced back across the paddies and found a corpsman who was tending another casualty. When the doc promised to finish and move up within a few minutes, Buchs returned to his squad. Marquardt was dead by the time help arrived.

Corporal O'Malley, still aboard the lead tank, poured rounds into the hedgerow on the left side, and Buchs opened fire at the hedgerow on the right, to suppress enemy fire. They tried tossing grenades into the thick growth, but these had little effect. The VC were in trenches on the other side of the hedgerows, and the grenades either bounced back or stuck in the bamboo growth before they reached their targets.

Buchs spotted a small opening in the hedgerow on the right and passed the word to O'Malley. "I'll cover you while you move through," Buchs shouted.

"Well, let's go, Buchs," came the reply. O'Malley, and then Buchs, went through the shrubbery, jumped into the trench, and carried the fight to the VC. Buchs took the left side while his squad leader took the right, and they overwhelmed a dozen of the enemy. O'Malley shot eight of them dead, and Buchs downed the other four.

The pair ran out of ammunition as other VC started down the trench toward them, so they jumped out of the trench and reloaded. Then they rolled back into the trench and resumed their assault. O'Malley called on Lance Corporal Hayden to check the bodies of the downed VC and ordered Rimpson, their M79 grenadier, to position himself at the opening of the trenchline.

As O'Malley went down the left side of the trench and Buchs gave him cover, a VC who was playing possum jumped up and threw a grenade at Hayden. Hayden leaped back and fell as Buchs killed the VC. Hayden was hit with a grenade fragment in the hip, and O'Malley took one in the foot. Buchs collected the VC weapons, then helped O'Malley get Hayden out of the trench.

Rimpson joined them in the trench and killed another advancing VC with his grenade launcher from about fifteen yards. The Marines were lucky that they were not hit, too, because they were well within the bursting radius of the round from Rimpson's M79.

They finished collecting the enemy weapons and loaded them on a tank to be taken to an LZ and evacuated by helicopter. Although wounded, O'Malley decided to stay with his men and refused to be evacuated.

CHAPTER 8

THE TAKING OF AN CUONG 2

An Cuong 2 was heavily wooded and fortified. Among its twenty-five to thirty huts were bunkers, trenchlines, and pillboxes. Most were covered over with logs and then with banana leaves to camouflage them.

As the India Company, 3/3, Marines moved toward the village the firing picked up again. A machine-gun team moved across a paddy and ran into a buzz saw of automatic weapons fire, probably a machine gun. Private First Class Howard Miller was the only survivor of his four-man team, from which Pfc Gilbert Nickerson, Pfc Walter Smith, and Pfc James White were all killed. As the junior man in the team, Miller carried his rifle and two hundred rounds of M60 machine-gun ammunition in a metal box. After his team members were lost, he slung his rifle over his back, carried the ammo box in one hand and the machine-gun in the other.

Miller looked for cover and spotted what seemed to be an artillery crater. When he leaped into the hole he accidentally smacked another Marine hard in the helmet with the ammunition box. The Marine interrupted Miller's apology with a command to stop worrying and keep digging. "We got to get deeper!"

Many Marines moved forward alongside rice paddies and an overgrown drainage ditch just outside of An Cuong 2. Several 60mm mortar rounds dropped among the attackers, but amid all the noise and confusion some of the Marines didn't believe they were really mortars.

Mortars are fearsome because they don't make much noise in flight. If you do not know they have been fired, they suddenly intrude on your world with explosions that hurtle dozens of hot, razor-sharp, life- and limb-taking fragments. Under the right conditions of range and relative noise level it might be possible to hear them leaving the tube. From that point it is usually a matter of wait and see. They are an indirect-fire weapon; the projectile travels in a high arc and, inasmuch they make little noise in flight, those on the ground have no indication where the rounds are going to impact. If they are heard leaving the tube, someone will usually yell, "Incoming!" and *everyone* will hit the deck, hopefully in a hole or behind something, and try to make themselves as small as possible. There is no real way to hide from a mortar. Their high angle of fire may bring them on your side of an obstacle rather than the enemy's side. Even being in a hole is no guarantee for survival as the rounds can, and have, found their way to the inside of deep holes and trenches. Knowing that mortar rounds are in the air in your general vicinity inspires a wide variety of fears, hopes, and "let's make a deal" with your God. For those untouched by an incoming barrage there is a great sense of "anybody but me" relief to hear the rounds impact and then know that you have bought another tenuous hold on life.

In this case, the action around them prevented the India Company, 3/3, Marines from hearing the mortars being fired. When Sgt Pat Finton pointed out a dud that landed nearby with the fins sticking up out of a rice paddy, everyone became a believer, said one version or another of "Oh, shit!" and jumped into the overgrown drainage ditch.

Engineers Pfc Glenn Johnson and Staff Sergeant Wilson, decided to take their chances in the open because of their experiences with finding booby traps in ditches. "FO up!" came a call from the front of the unit, where an artillery forward observer was needed. Wilson fell back to guide the FO forward. Mortars burst among them again with renewed intensity and this time the engineers thought that maybe getting into the trench wasn't such a bad idea after all. All around them Marines were digging in and hugging the ground.

After the Marines had dug for about twenty minutes and put some fire out to their front, enemy activity trailed off. The India Company Marines got up to resume the attack.

The intensity of the fighting rose and fell for no discernible reasons. Sometimes it seemed to be going on all sides at once. At other moments, there was very little gunfire at all.

The Marines quickly learned a practical lesson that all warriors have known since ancient times. Theoretically, one is supposed to line up in an assault or other planned formation and fight that way. But once battle is joined the formation rapidly degenerates into a series of isolated small actions. In Starlite, as in most battles, it seemed that the fights generally meant that four or five men on one side would be heavily engaged with a similar number on the opposite side. Each combatant became so preoccupied with taking care of his situation that he often had little knowledge of and didn't really care what was going on a few yards away. Throw in the sounds, the smells, and the fear and you have the notorious "fog of war" that explains why such widely differing accounts describe the same battle.

Amidst this chaos and mayhem, Capt Bruce Webb seemed to be everywhere. The popular skipper repeatedly exposed himself to urge his men forward, give orders, and call for supporting arms.

While preparing for the attack on the village itself, Captain Webb had radioed for close air support. The Marines could not get radio contact with the direct air support center (DASC) in Chulai, so the two forward air controllers (FACs), Captain Dalby and Lieutenant Schwend, spoke to the pilots directly, calling them in by their plane numbers. They could tell what ordnance loads the aircraft were carrying by looking at them. The F4 Phantoms and A4 Skyhawks circling the area were loaded with fragmentation bombs and napalm, and they were directed against targets as needed by the men on the ground. Although the by-the-book members of the DASC were horrified at the procedure, the result was an impressive bit of innovative close air support coordination between the pilots and the ground troops. The forward air controllers also managed to coordinate with the artillery people and notify pilots when the ordinate of artillery was going to exceed 2,000 feet in the area through which Marine aircraft were going to fly.

Marine FACs are Marine aviators. The Corps had learned in World War II that the best air support coordination was between a pilot on the ground and a pilot in the air.

The turn-around time for A4s and F4s was very short. Danang, where the F4s were based, was only about fifty miles away; and the A4s were based right there, at Chulai. Their target area during Starlite was practically in the traffic pattern for the airstrip. The limiting factor for the A4s was how fast they could land, rearm, and take off again. Seventy-eight fixed-wing sorties were flown in support of the operation, most of them on the first day. The Phantoms and Skyhawks expended 65 tons of bombs, 4 tons of napalm, 533 2.75-inch rockets, and 6,000 rounds of 20mm ammo. In excess of 500 helicopter sorties were flown, and 3 KC-130 transport aircraft from Marine Transport Squadron 152 were engaged in evacuating the dead and wounded from Chulai to Danang.

As the Marine aircraft came in on An Cuong 2, the VC darted out of their positions and shot at the planes, and the Marines on the ground opened fire on the VC. When the planes left, the VC scurried back into their hiding places, and the ground Marines were left without clear targets. This happened several times, and inasmuch as the firing was wild—no one seemed to take aim—the effectiveness of the small arms on either side was doubtful.

During one of the strikes a number of Marines moved to the backside of the hill for a cigarette break. Bomb fragments whistled by and forced these Marines to seek cover in a wooded area where the hot, sharp missiles thunked into the trees. The bombs wounded several India Company Marines, among them Corporals Walker and Thomas, who both refused evacuation.

Most Marines hugged the ground, but one thought that he would like a piece of bomb fragment for a souvenir. He grasped a shard about 6 inches long to pull it from a tree but quickly dropped it when he discovered that fragments from newly exploded ordnance are blistering hot.

Colonel Muir's insistence that his people master supporting arms fire paid off in spades. The Marines knew that naval gunfire was a flat-trajectory weapon. This meant that the high arc associated with land-based artillery was absent and thus reduced the time between when they could call naval gunfire and air support. This permitted them to keep continuous pressure on the enemy force, which sustained enormous casualties.

*   *   *

As Pfc Chuck Fink passed through a field he felt that there was something strange about it. His squad stopped moving and he noticed there was a rise in the ground, maybe five or six feet high, twenty to thirty feet wide, and maybe several hundred meters long. He spotted a perfectly round hole in the side of this mound. When he went over and looked, he saw the tail fin of a mortar round sticking out of it. He didn't know whether to push the round in or pull it out. It dawned on him that this might be a ventilation shaft for a bunker complex.

Fink called over Sgt George Emerick to tell him what he had found. At this point in the battle many of the enemy seemed to have disappeared and Fink thought that they have gone to ground in this bunker. He wanted to call in an air strike on it, but before he could get word of his find up to the company commander his squad was ordered forward. They no sooner passed over the area than the VC poured heavy fire on them from the rear.

When Fink's squad was sent back to suppress the enemy activity he found himself walking point with Pfc John Jemison, an M79 grenadier. The two of them hit the deck and rolled out from behind a paddy dike to take a look. Fink spotted a machine gun about fifty yards away that was chewing up the company. The VC had not yet seen the two Marines even though they were firing over their heads. The machine-gun position was very well camouflaged, and even though Fink could see it, Jemison couldn't make it out inside the foliage. Fink told Jemison that he would fire a rifle round right beneath the machine gun to mark the target so Jemison could take them out with his grenade launcher.

As soon as Fink got a round off, Jemison shouted happily that he had the target, and he quickly fired his M79. The very first round Jemison fired in combat appeared to hit the enemy gunner right in the middle of the helmet and take out part of the VC gun crew. But Jemison's fire gave his position away to the surviving VC. Jemison rolled over to reload, and as he did a VC jumped on the gun and loosed a burst in his direction. Jemsion was hit in the head and died instantly. Fink shot the second VC gunner, at which point the other three members of the machine-gun squad jumped up to run away. Chuck Fink shot all of them dead.

From somewhere to Fink's left a VC grenadier launched an RPG at him. The missile spent most of its destructive power on the paddy dike to Fink's front, and much of the rest on his rifle stock, which shattered and sent some fragments into Fink's face and forearm. The blast turned Fink over on his back, which he thought was almost comical.

Here he was, lying on his back with his helmet blown around backwards and his eyeglasses cocked up on his head. After a few seconds he sobered up enough to straighten his glasses and helmet, and to try to stop the bleeding in his arm.

Fink's squad leader, Corporal Jones, came over and asked, "Are you okay?" Fink replied that he was dinged a little but added, "I think John Jemison is dead." Jones replied that Jemison was very dead as he started to put a battle dressing on Fink's arm. Jones was kneeling to work on Fink when suddenly he flinched and calmly said, "I think I just got shot in the shoulder." This struck Fink as very strange. He wondered if a man wouldn't know for sure that he was shot. He looked at Jones, and sure enough the squad leader had been shot in the shoulder. There was no exit wound; the round was still in him. Fink took Jones's battle dressing and made a sling out of it for him. By this time Fink's own hand was beginning to stiffen and had become difficult to use.

*   *   *

As Pfc Howard Miller moved forward again and prepared to jump a trench a VC heaved a Chicom grenade at him. Miller was untouched by the grenade fragments, but the blast blew him back against the side of the trench and knocked the wind out of him. After a moment he decided he wasn't hurt, struggled to his feet, and jumped over the trench again to resume his charge.

Bruce Webb was everywhere throughout the action, leading the assault of his company. He impressed all with his calm demeanor and courage.

The India Company 3/3 assault elements seized and occupied the village. More than forty of the enemy died in the taking of An Cuong 2.

WITH O'MALLEY. 1100

The tanks with Cpl Robert O'Malley's squad were targeted by anti-armor fire and one of the vehicles was hit. The other tanks directed their fire toward the enemy position and either hit the enemy weapon or discouraged the VC crew from using it further. As soon as O'Malley's Marines got the wounded loaded on the tanks they resumed their advance. They were moving well when, for some reason, the tanks stopped. In an instant the enemy was on them again with small arms and crew-served weapons. Putting the wounded Marines on the tanks had not been a great idea. The VC saw them more easily, and many were hit again.

The tanks bunched up in an effort to protect the damaged tank they had with them. Corporal O'Malley jumped into the bushes and pointed out targets to the tank crews, but small-arms fire from the right flank forced the Marines back into the trenchline. When several mortar rounds landed among the tanks the vehicles started to back up. The Marines in the trench knew that as the tanks retreated they were going to draw the enemy mortars into the trench with them.

Lance Corporal Chris Buchs looked at O'Malley and said, "We'd better move out of here!" O'Malley agreed, but it was nearly too late. As the two exited the trench a barrage of mortar rounds hit a few yards away and blew them both back to the bottom. O'Malley came up from the trench with a second wound, a mortar fragment lodged in his forearm. He began to move his troops back.

In the confusion, Buchs lost track of O'Malley and asked Pfc Robert Rimpson where he was. Rimpson reported that he had last seen O'Malley return to the trench. Buchs and Rimpson ran forward once more and found O'Malley, who ignored both of his own wounds to pick up another wounded Marine. The young corporal ordered Buchs and Rimpson to pick up yet another wounded man, and they all continued to move back.

INDIA SIX DOWN. 1000.

At this time Lt Richard Purnell, the India Company executive officer, got a report that O'Malley's squad, now several hundred meters down the trenchline, had some casualties. He moved a small group to where the tanks were and began the process of getting the wounded people evacuated. At the time, there was no more fire near the trenchline, but the Marines saw several VC take off into a village to the north.

Having suppressed the enemy fire in and around An Cuong 2, India Company was able to move across the streambed cross the trenchline, and come up onto a flat spot. Staff Sergeant Jean Pinquet was going through the area, putting bullets into the heads of the VC on the ground with his .45 pistol, to make sure they were dead. Word had it that Pinquet was either a former French Foreign Legionnaire or had been in the French Resistance in World War II. Whatever his past, he was regarded as being a very tough Marine. Captain Webb ordered him to stop shooting the VC, saying it was inhumane.

Private First Class Glenn Johnson was a few feet from Captain Webb, who was talking on the radio, when he saw a flash of light. Johnson yelled, "Grenade!" swung his arm out, and hit Pfc Freddy Link, who was right behind him; he swept himself and Link backward into a trench. When the two got back up they found that the captain and his radio operator were both down.

One of the VC who was thought to be dead had rolled over and thrown a grenade at the India Company command group. The Marines quickly killed the enemy soldier, but Webb and other Marines were nonetheless casualties.

Directly to the left was a brick chimney-like structure that was about three and a half feet high and two and a half feet square. As Johnson walked up, two young Vietnamese men popped up out of the brick structure. Johnson was going to shoot them when someone hollered, "Don't shoot, take them as prisoners." The Vietnamese men had no visible arms and were in civilian clothing, so the Marines hauled them out and tied them up. When they turned back to the CP group, people were working on Webb and the other Marine casualties.

First Sergeant Petty, who beelined to see what was going on, ran into Gunnery Sergeant Martin, who had been wounded by the grenade blast. Martin told the first sergeant that the skipper was lying next to a small tree and that he knew the captain was dead, but he had nonetheless told the troops that Webb was still alive but wounded. Petty went to look at his CO. All he could see of Webb's chest was bathed in blood.

About this time the medevac chopper was trying to land in a very small clearing on the southeast corner of An Cuong 2. No one was helping, so Petty ran over and directed him in with arm signals.

As Maj Al Bloom brought his aircraft in for the medevac he was amazed to see a Marine standing upright amid the fire, guiding him in with hand and arm signals. Bloom screamed, uselessly, for the Marine to get down. It didn't occur to him at the time that his helicopter was a far more lucrative target for the VC than a lone Marine. At about twelve feet of altitude, Bloom looked down and was shocked to see that he was about to set down on the chest of one of the casualties. Fueled by adrenaline, Bloom pulled the bird over and landed to the left of the wounded Marine.

The medevac, originally called for the earlier casualties, had landed and another had been called for as soon as the grenade went off. Private First Class Johnson joined in to pick up Captain Webb's stretcher to take him to the chopper. Webb was on his back, and was carried head-first toward the chopper. Johnson, who was on the captain's left, saw that Webb's right arm lay across his stomach. The young Marine thought the captain was dead because he had a big slash across his right arm that was not bleeding.

The courageous, well-liked, and energetic skipper, who had so fearlessly led his men this day, had been ashore less than four hours. He was to be posthumously awarded the Navy Cross Medal for his actions.

Johnson looked up and saw first sergeant's stripes on one of the other stretcher-bearers. It was 1stSgt Art Petty. Johnson thought "What is the first sergeant doing out here?" Some first sergeants, figuring that they had paid their dues, did not get that close to a fight; they took care of administrative matters in the rear. But Petty, an experienced World War II combat veteran with three major landings against the Japanese under his belt, could be counted on to be near the action.

Bruce Webb was the first dead Marine Johnson ever saw. Like most Marines, Johnson was too busy to let it keep him from his job, so the reality didn't sink in until later. He liked Webb, whom he thought always got the job done but took no unnecessary risks with his men. A superb Marine officer, Webb had carried himself well, respected all the people around him, and took good care of his Marines. Private First Class Gary Hammet lamented, "We lost our captain, we lost a radio operator, and we lost a private. If it hadn't been for the captain telling the staff sergeant to quit what he was doing, Captain Webb might be alive today. Captain Webb was a good man who wouldn't tell you to do what he wouldn't do. So that was the end of Captain Webb."

Not all the India Company Marines wanted to believe that Webb had been killed. After he was hit and before he was evacuated a Marine took the captain's .45 pistol and said, "This is my company commander's, and I am keeping it for him."

*   *   *

The dead and wounded, dressed in blood-soaked bandages, were carried on stretchers or ponchos to the makeshift LZ, where the corpsmen and their comrades worked on them. Art Petty supervised the loading of the chopper with the badly wounded. He tried to get one of the India Company NCOs, Corporal Reed, who was full of holes, on one of the birds, but the pilot waved him off, saying he was already overloaded. Reed laid there and gamely reassured Petty, "Don't worry, Top, I'll catch the next one." He did get out on the next helicopter and survived.

While Petty was busy with medevacs, gunfire erupted to his left. He looked over and saw a bunch of Viet Cong trying to get into a hole in an embankment at the same time. Marines about twenty feet to their rear were shooting them in the back.

Lieutenant Richard Purnell, who was still tending to casualties down the trenchline, expected a medevac helicopter any minute. Fifteen or twenty minutes later a helicopter did land back in the vicinity of An Cuong 2, took off, and left. The lieutenant couldn't quite understand what the problem was. A few minutes later another helicopter flew into the area to pick up his casualties.

A wounded Marine on the chopper brought the unwelcome news that the company commander had been hit and evacuated. Also, the Marine said, the company gunny, the artillery forward observer, and two of the radio operators had been killed or wounded. Lieutenant Purnell was new to India Company, 3/3, and did not know the platoon or squad leaders that well; he had not seen that much action, was on the first major operation of the war, and his captain had just gotten killed. More was to come. It was a tremendous burden for a relatively inexperienced officer; he was now in command of the company, and the company was not in an enviable spot. But Purnell was up to the challenge; he was awarded the Silver Star Medal for his actions this day.

*   *   *

Following the medevacs, India Company moved out to outskirts of An Cuong 2, where it encountered sporadic fire as it turned a bit to the right and went down a trail.

Lieutenant Purnell notified the battalion commander that his skipper had been killed, that he was in charge, and what the situation was. They had run into quite a bit of enemy activity but that seemed to be tapering off, and the company was receiving hardly any fire at all at present. Lieutenant Colonel Muir ordered Purnell to turn his India Company back to the north and join up with the rest of the battalion.

NAM YEN 3. 1130

After it had secured Hill 43, 1stLt Mike Jenkins's Hotel Company, 2/4, renewed its drive toward Nam Yen 3. Automatic weapons fire from a house near Hill 43 started to pester the Marines. An M48 tank moved over to get a shot at the house, but an anti-armor weapon hit the tank. A second tank moved over to shoot at the house. It was also hit, but it destroyed the house and put an end to the small-arms fire emanating from that sector. Neither tank was damaged severely and they both were back in action within minutes.

Next, a heavy volume of Viet Cong fire tore into the Marines from a hedgerow southeast of Hill 43. A flame tank rumbled over to the position, discharged its flamethrower on the hedgerow, and burned it up.

The 1st Platoon and two tanks threw in a coordinated tank-infantry attack to relieve pressure on the 2d Platoon, which was pinned by automatic and small arms fire as well as 82mm and 60mm mortar fire.

Corporal Dick Tonucci worked his way over, climbed onto the back of one of the tanks, and grabbed the tank-infantry phone on the back of the vehicle. He talked the tank in the direction from which the heaviest .51-caliber machine-gun fire was coming. A large-caliber round slammed into the tank, badly damaged it, and propelled Tonucci through the air into a water-filled paddy. The tank's fuel cells were ruptured and began burning. When the tank was inspected the next day it was found that the engine compartment was completely gutted; the right track was burned off; the air cleaners, stowage boxes, and fenders were fused together; and the radio was melted in a solid mass. Although the 90mm ammunition had not cooked off, the bases of the shell cases were swollen over the ends of the rack hold-downs. The M48 was not repairable, so engineers destroyed it in place. It remains there to this day.

Tonucci left the flaming vehicle and took off down a trench to the right to try and get to the enemy gun. He left LCpl Corporal J. C. Paul to protect wounded Marines. Paul was wounded himself, and had actually been aboard a medevac chopper, but when he saw help was needed he had jumped off the helicopter and gone back to the fight.

Now a group of VC was trying to get to the casualties lying on the ground to finish them off. Tonucci had his hands full with the enemy machine gun, but he thought that if he could neutralize it, Hotel

Company could move to its objective. He yelled at Paul to protect the wounded Marines while he concentrated his own efforts on the gun.

A group of Viet Cong started down the trench toward Tonucci. Chasing them was the flame tank, which spat a stream of napalm at the enemy. A bunch of small burning men jumped out of the trench and was shot down by Marines in the vicinity.

The flame tank was also coming straight at Tonucci, preceded by its tongue of fiery death. Tonucci shot out of the trench like a scalded cat, barely avoiding the intense flames, and continued after the enemy machine gun. As he closed on the gun position he heard something snap behind him. He turned, ready to fire. Luckily he didn't, because it was Pfc Ronny Centers, who had come up to support him. The two of them took out a grenade launcher in a bunker, the machine-gun bunker, and another bunker beside it. When a back-up crew for the machine gun popped out of the ground and manned the weapon, Tonucci and Centers killed them, too. Before they were through, the two Marines had killed fourteen of the VC. The tank crew recommended them both for Silver Star Medals for conspicuous gallantry, which they later received.

In the meantime, Lance Corporal Paul's attempt to protect the wounded was coming under heavy pressure. On top of the fire from mortars, recoilless rifles, and small arms, the Viet Cong added a barrage of white phosphorous. (WP) rifle grenades. WP burns with an intense heat and will continue to burn, even under water, until it consumes itself. It easily burns through human flesh. Paul raced across the paddy, placed himself in an exposed position between the casualties and the enemy, and poured out a torrent of automatic rifle fire in order to divert the enemy long enough to permit the casualties to be evacuated. Tenaciously protecting the casualties in the face of certain death, he was hit several times but refused to quit until the wounded were pulled to safety. After the other casualties were safe, Tonucci picked up Paul and put him on a medevac chopper. He hoped that Paul would live, but the fearless Marine didn't make it. Joe Calvin Paul, the quiet kid from Kentucky, was posthumously awarded the Medal of Honor, and the U.S. Navy later named a frigate, the USS *Paul* (FF 1080) in his honor.

*   *   *

The tank-infantry attack caused the VC to break contact and fall back to the west. Mike Jenkins called in an air strike to hit the fleeing enemy and, having finally secured the hill, led his company back toward Nam Yen 3. In addition to killing a lot of Viet Cong, Lieutenant Jenkins's Marines captured a prisoner and collected more than forty weapons from the carefully camouflaged bunkers in the hedgerows.

O'MALLEY. 1130

As Cpl Robert O'Malley and the survivors of his squad made their way to rejoin India Company they saw other Marines from the company come in to break up a circle the VC were trying to form around them. There were Marine casualties in the open, so O'Malley once again put himself in harm's way. He led his men out into the rice paddies where they were subjected to another mortar barrage. This time O'Malley caught a fragment in the chest, which punctured a lung. Lance Corporal Chris Buchs could see that O'Malley was hurt, but the squad leader kept moving; he got the dead Marines loaded onto the tanks. Sometime during the action Pfc Robert Rimpson caught a piece of shell fragment near his eye, which was popped out of its socket. He pushed it back into his head, but Rimpson thereafter had a hard time with his vision.

By the time O'Malley's squad got inside the India Company perimeter, the company had set up a solid position. Buchs got O'Malley and Rimpson to sit down and tried to treat their wounds. The company's wounded received some rudimentary medical attention they moved to an LZ for pickup.

*   *   *

Medevac birds from two Marine squadrons were inbound, but they couldn't land because of enemy fire. There appeared to be a .30-caliber machine gun on a nearby hill that was keeping the helicopters at bay. HMM-361's Lt Dick Hooton decided to go in. He radioed, "This is Tarbrush [his radio callsign] aircraft rolling in, rolling in." Another HMM-361 aircraft followed Hooton into the LZ. Lieutenant Hooton was not even supposed to be there. He was assigned that day as the squadron maintenance test officer, but because his fellow aviators Ramsey Myatt, Bud Sanders, and Stu Kendall had been wounded he had joined the fight.

As Hooton's helicopter touched down, O'Malley's Marines were still going after a .30-caliber machine gun that had tried to prevent the helicopters from landing. Rimpson attempted to get it with his M79, but he couldn't focus with his damaged eye, so the rounds went over the target. After a few misses, Buchs took Rimpson's weapon and got the machine gun on his second shot. Corporal O'Malley, despite his three wounds, fired at the hill the whole time.

There were about fifteen casualties to be evacuated when Hooton and the other helicopter landed. The second helicopter to land was the first one loaded, and O'Malley once again refused evacuation until all the others were aboard.

Seven Marines went out on the first load as O'Malley and the rest of India Company kept fire on the VC-held hill. After the other helicopter took off O'Malley and the rest of his squad boarded Lieutenant Hooton's bird.

About the time it took off and the Marines aboard relaxed a bit, LCpl Chris Buchs felt that something was wrong with his chest. He looked down and was astonished to see that he had been wounded.

The helicopter took a hit and lost some of its hydraulic power. The airplane went for the USS *Iwo Jima,* but the helicopter carrier tried to wave Hooten off because of the damage. Lieutenant Hooton responded that he had nowhere else to go, declared a Mayday situation, and put down with all hands safely delivered.

The wounded were taken to sickbay for immediate treatment. As soon as O'Malley's men were patched up they went to find out what had happened to him. They found the doctor who had treated his wounds, and he said O'Malley would be okay. Sixteen months later, in Austin, Texas, President Lyndon Johnson presented to Robert Emmett O'Malley with the first Medal of Honor to be awarded to a Marine in the Vietnam War.

*   *   *

Later in the day Lt Dick Hooten's H-34 was again badly shot up, but he made it back to Chulai with an A4 attack aircraft as escort. Hooton's co-pilot, Lt Ken Slowey, was slightly wounded in the arm, and his crew chief, Corporal Ely, lost a toe. Even so, Hooton got another aircraft and went back to work. He received the Distinguished Flying Cross for his heroism that day.

Many helicopters were hit by enemy fire this day. Of the eighteen in HMM-361 that were available for duty at the beginning of the day, fourteen were hit. More than half of these sustained damage that normally would have grounded them, but somehow they struggled back to base, where repair crews cannibalized those that had been hit worst to keep the others flying. As regular crewmen became casualties, volunteers jumped in to fill their places.

Operation Starlite

Photo Gallery

A CH-46 unloads marines in the initial airlift. *NA*

U.S. Navy Seabees construct the new Chulai
airstrip in blistering heat. *USMC*

Brigadier General Keith McCutcheon greets Col. John Noble, the CO of Marine Aircraft Group 12 after the latter landed the first aircraft at the new Chulai base. *USMC*

A patrol from 2/4 fords a deep stream in the area around Chulai. *USMC*

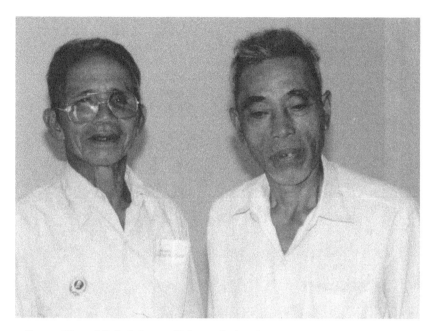

Duong Hong Minh, left, set off the explosive charge on Green Beach as India Company 3/3 came ashore. Then he and Phan Tan Huan, right, fought a delaying action to keep the Marines away from their regimental CP. *Author*

Tranh Ngoc Trung's 60th VC Battalion was the main opposition on LZ Blue. *Author*

Dinh The Pham, vice commander of 40th Battalion, 1st VC Regiment. A veteran of Dien Bien Phu, his service began in 1944 with the Viet Minh. *Author*

(Left) Nguyen Van Ngoc, head of the Da Nang veterans' group. *Author*

(Below right) Tran Nhu Tiep, of the 60th Battalion, 1st VC Regiment, that bedeviled Hotel Company 2/4 at LZ Blue. *Author*

(Left) Major Andy Comer XO of 3/3. *Photo courtesy of Comer*

(Below) Marines from 2/4 sweep past a hamlet in Operation Starlite. *USMC*

An Ontos patrols the beach past some Vietnamese fishing boats on Operation Starlite. *USMC*

Echo Company, 2/4 moves out from LZ White immediately after landing in Operation Starlite. *USMC*

A MAG-16 helicopter (below) evacuates casualties while a Marine M–48 tank stands guard during *Operation Starlite.* The marine on the left is carrying an M–79 grenade launcher. *USMC*

A Marine helicopter from HMM-361 brings ammunition to a howtar position during *Operation Starlite.* The howtar is a 107mm. mortar tube mounted on a pack howitzer chassis (hence the name). *USMC*

General Lew Walt, left, congratulates Colonel Oscar Peatross and Lieutenant Colonel Charles Bodleyon the success of Starlite. *USMC*

Vietnamese cemetery near the Starlite battlefield. Like most of these cemeteries through out Vietnam, the graves are empty or are arranged around a mass grave. They are meant to be memorials of certain battles. *Author*

Sergeant Ernie Wallace receives the Navy Cross Medal from Lieutenant General James Masters. *USMC*

The cupola of the tank destroyed during *Operation Starlite*. The Vietnamese have constructed a war memorial around it. *Author*

Hill 43 as it looks today. *Author*

CHAPTER 9

HEAVY FIGHTING ON ALL FRONTS

HOTEL, 2/4. 1130

At 1130, Hotel Company, 2/4's attack on Nam Yen 3 began afresh with the 2d Platoon on the right, the 3d Platoon on the left, and the 1st Platoon as rear guard. As the company moved toward the village the two remaining tanks positioned themselves immediately behind the assault platoons and the three Ontos moved to cover the rear and the flanks in general support. The rice paddies in this area were flooded, making it difficult for the tracked vehicles to traverse them.

When the 2d and 3d platoons reached the stream and rice paddies east of Nam Yen 3, the 1st Platoon, was struck by heavy automatic fire from its rear as well as the company's eastern flank.

The 2d and 3d Platoons immediately encountered a serious threat of their own, first in the form of small arms fire and then from 82mm and 60mm mortars. The two platoons quickly moved across the paddies and set up a defense near the southern end of An Cuong 2. The tanks and Ontos were stymied in their attempt to join them via the flooded paddies. No adequate route could be located, so the Ontos attempted to cross in trace of the troops. The first made it across, but the second became mired in the mud. A third Ontos pulled the trapped one from the muck under heavy fire.

During this time the crescendo of incoming mortar and small arms fire was reinforced by the addition of anti-armor weapons from the vicinity of Hill 30, an eastward promontory that provided the VC there with a clear view of the field Hotel Company was crossing. The three Ontos tried to find a way out of the field, but there was mud in every direction and the berms of the paddy were so high that the Marines could not see over them. The two outside vehicles were hit and the radio in the center Ontos was knocked out.

The vehicle commander, Cpl Robert "Frenchie" Bousquat, opened the hatchway and, ignoring the fire, stood up in his vehicle to get a better view of the terrain, to look for a way out of the paddy. He took a round through the helmet, and then he was shot directly in the chest. He said to his driver, "I'm going to die soon," but continued to stand tall in the vehicle hatchway, exposed to fire, until he spotted an exit and led all three vehicles through. Then he collapsed and died. As Bousquat had trained him to do, LCpl Thomas Spradling pushed the young man's body aside and took command of the Ontos.

In the direction of the village, 1stLt Mike Jenkins's men came upon a VC-occupied trench about twelve feet deep, three feet wide at bottom, and approximately twelve feet wide at top. It had been filled with punji stakes, sharp pieces of bamboo meant to disable the unwary attacker. The Hotel Company Marines assaulted the trench and drove the enemy off.

Since the ditch was too wide to jump, the Marines had to go down one side and vault up the other. Lieutenant Jenkins's radio operator, Pfc Jim Scott, was tripped up by one of the punji stakes in the trench; it ripped his trousers from the cuff to belt buckle. Scott did not get a scratch, but he spent the rest of the operation with his butt hanging out.

Jenkins took advantage of the brief respite provided by the cover of the trench to bring his platoon commanders together and give them a fragmentary attack order for taking the village. He held back no reserve, because Hotel Company was getting fire from all directions.

Afraid to wait too long in case the enemy had the trench zeroed in by indirect-fire weapons, Jenkins gave the signal and everyone climbed out of the trench on a line and advanced toward the village. The distance from the ditch to the edge of the five acres of woods in which the houses of the village were scattered was about one hundred and fifty feet. The Marines were ordered to move into the trees on the edge of the village.

As they approached the village some of the VC filtered out of spider holes and bunkers to try to get behind the Marines. One of the platoons changed direction a little to counter the enemy movement. Many Marines became separated from their squads and platoons and, in small groups, headed into a large drainage ditch near the trees that was deep enough to stand up in without getting one's head blown off. Conspicuous among the junior troop leaders, Sgt Jerry Tharp was barking orders, trying to sort things out. Here and there were rickety bamboo fences across the trench, interlaced with barbed wire that slowed Hotel Company's advance. Out of nowhere, the Marines came upon a group of South Vietnamese Popular Forces crouched together in the trench. These allies were dressed in new uniforms and had better field gear than the Marines. The Marines motioned to them to follow, but the Vietnamese were not interested in getting involved in the fight. The Marines continued on.

The Popular Forces were a sort of a village militia. They were minimally trained and, given the uncertain loyalties of many of the Vietnamese, not credited with being especially trustworthy. The fact that they were even present in a Viet Cong stronghold should have alerted the Marines. At a point in the fight when things seemed to be going against Hotel Company, several of them removed their distinctive red neck scarves and opened fire on Lieutenant Jenkins's men. Machine-gunner Cpl Edward Vaughn and others Marines quickly and savagely responded in kind, killing those who fired on them.

There was a lot of yelling and confusion, and about that time Pfc Dick Boggia looked around to try to locate his gunner, LCpl Ken Stankiewicz. Boggia called out to learn if anyone had seen Stankiewicz, but no one had.

As the Hotel Company Marines made their way forward there was heavy fighting all round, especially to the right, toward Hill 43. As they approached the end of the ditch they came under immediate, intense, and very accurate fire.

VC snipers were very good at their trade; they exacted a toll among the Marines caught in the open. A number of Marines who had reached cover, such as Dick Tonucci, left safety and moved to where they could support the withdrawal of their fellows.

Private First Class Dick Boggia was pinned up against a dike by sniper fire from both front and rear, trying to figure out how he was going to get out of there.

Among those pinned down was Corporal Spurrier, a fire team leader. He was both exposed and out of ammunition. His automatic rifleman, Pfc Robert Lee Stipes, decided to get him back. Stipes was a self-described country boy who hadn't seen much of the world and had a problem with authority. He had lost a stripe more than once because of his unmilitary attitude. He proved what he was made of this day when he charged out onto an open paddy and laid down a ferocious volume of fire that permitted Spurrier and others to withdraw to relative safety. For this, and for later evacuating casualties under fire, he was awarded the Bronze Star Medal.

Sergeant Jerry Tharp yelled for the Marines to fan out along the back of a small berm adjacent to a dirt road that ran parallel to the village complex and prepare to renew the assault. While speaking with Lieutenant Jenkins in preparation for the new attack, Tharp raised his head to take a final look. He was immediately hit. Blood instantly appeared below his neck and cascaded down his chest. He made a feeble attempt to take his gear off and get to his wound before he just, in the words of Lieutenant Jenkins, "melted and collapsed before my eyes." Blood poured from his mouth, and he was dead. From the angle of his wound it was apparent that a sniper in a tree shot him.

It was about this time, too, that Hotel Company lost its gunnery sergeant, Al Raitt. Gunny Raitt was a colorful veteran of World War II and Korea who was described by one Marine as the only man he ever knew who could chew Red Man tobacco and drink coffee at the same time. Raitt carried a shotgun on the operation, but at one point he decided he needed something with a little more range. He traded his scattergun with Jim Scott, Jenkins's radioman, for the latter's M14. He was standing on the edge of a ditch, firing furiously at the enemy, when he was gunned down and killed.

Snipers in trees were causing a great deal of damage. One of them seemed to take someone down with almost every round. When a Marine went down with a shot through the cheek, Tonucci and John "Rabbit" Slaughter went after his tormentor. Slaughter, called "Rabbit" because of his small size and good speed, was loaded for bear. He had lost a lot of weight since coming to Vietnam, and at the time of this operation was down to about a hundred pounds. The little Marine was a tough hard-charger who nearly carried his own weight in gear, much of it ammunition for his single-shot M79 grenade launcher. He had started the day with seventy-two M-79 rounds, which weigh eight ounces apiece, so he was carrying thirty-six pounds of ammunition when he started. He was resupplied with equal amounts three or four times during the day. The barrel of his weapon was worn and, in his words, "gleamed like gold." It made an enticing target. He had been breaking the shotgun-like action of his M79 and firing as fast as he could since he had come into the landing zone. About an hour into the battle he was struck by fragments from an enemy recoilless rifle round. The bits of hot metal peppered his face and he sustained one particularly bad cut beneath his left eye. Rabbit was hard man; he allowed the corpsman to put a bit of gauze on the cut and went right back to work with his weapon, staying in the field the entire day. Somehow he was left off the list to receive a Purple Heart for his wounds. The medal finally caught up with him in 1997, thirty-two years later.

Rabbit Slaughter's wounds were the least of his concerns at the time. He had plenty of targets, everywhere. *Everywhere!* With Tonucci covering for him and spotting his shots, Rabbit popped rounds up into the treetops, one at a time. This one sniper was still causing a lot of damage and needed to be taken out. Slaughter was down to his last two missiles when he got their man. The VC screamed upon being hit. He was tied in, so he only fell part way and dangled upside down from his knees while his unseeing eyes stared at the battle that continued without him.

It was at about this time that LCpl Ernie Wallace noticed that a large number of small pine trees were in fact camouflaged Viet Cong. He yelled to Tonucci, "Trees! Start killing trees!" Sure enough, the "trees" were well-concealed enemy, and when the Marines opened up on them many VC fell dead, others fired back, and still more of them scattered. Tonucci's squad shot most of them to death. Ernie Wallace once more proved his prowess with the M60 machine gun by accounting for at least fifteen VC KIA. This brought his number of kills for the day to more than forty.

At one point when a medevac chopper came in Wallace ran over and demanded that the crew chief trade machine guns. The bipod had been shot off Wallace's gun, and it had other damage. The crew chief didn't like it very much, but Wallace was bigger and had a determined look about him that decided the issue. The swap was made.

As busy as he was, Wallace found time to tend to Pfc Jim Mazy, who had some shell fragments in his ear and chin. Wallace's aggressive heroism and expertise with his gun, and in getting wounded Marines out, earned him the Navy Cross Medal.

Private First Class Dick Boggia finally found LCpl Ken Stankiewicz, who had been wounded in the arm. He told Boggia to take care of the gun. He seemed to be okay and he was placed on a tank for medevac. Putting the wounded on the tanks turned out to be a poor idea. They became fire magnets. Stankiewicz was hit again, this time fatally.

Private Sam Badnek was another of those men who had a problem with authority. The fact that he was still a private at the time of Starlite was a testament to his inability to stay out of trouble. But Badnek was no slouch when it came to facing down a deadly enemy. While stationed in Hawaii he had had a parrot tattooed on his arm. As his platoon moved past Nam Yen 3, Badnek got hit in the parrot and also suffered a head wound. This turned out to be too much for the young Marine. He took off after an enemy bunker behind a hurricane of fire and single-handedly destroyed it and all its occupants. No one who witnessed his heroism had any idea how Badnek managed to survive the enemy's return fire. When Badnek was later awarded the Navy Cross Medal for conspicuous gallantry under fire he was still a private.

The 1st Platoon moved one squad around to the northwest of Nam Yen 3 and killed nine VC who were operating an 82mm mortar. The small arms fire then became so intense that the squad was driven back, closer to the tanks, and the Marines were unable to capture the enemy mortar.

Corporal Edward Vaughn spotted another enemy mortar team dashing for a wood line. He quickly deployed his M60 and shot the last three of them in line. Vaughn's aggressive deployment of his weapon the entire day inflicted great damage on the enemy. His gallantry in action this day was to win him a Silver Star Medal.

Under this intense fire courageous helicopter pilots lifted out some of the killed and wounded. Other casualties were loaded on tanks, which began to pull back toward LZ Blue.

HOTEL, 2/4. 1400

Lieutenant Mike Jenkins kept up the pressure on the enemy. While evacuating the wounded he called in artillery on Nam Yen 3 and ordered air strikes on the high ground at Hill 30, from whence Hotel was receiving so much grief earlier. For all that Hotel had bled, LtCol Bull Fisher ordered the company back to LZ Blue. At 1400 the battered unit, with all its attachments, began its march to the zone with Chris Cooney's 1st Platoon as the point and the 2d and 3d Platoons in the rear, fighting a delaying action.

In the confusion of the movement Sgt Jerry Tharp's body was left behind. Sergeant Juan Moreno selected four people and told them to drop their packs, grab a poncho, and go back for Tharp. The Marines found his body two to three hundred yards back along the trail, picked him up, and carried him out. It is one of the oldest Marine traditions that they never abandon their wounded or dead.

As Cooney's Marines opened their withdrawal movement, they were pinned behind a dike by small arms fire from Nam Yen 3 and from the southeast corner of An Cuong 2. At this time the 3d Platoon cut across the rice paddy in front of Hill 30, from which the VC fled. Cooney's platoon and some men from the 2d Platoon became separated from the rest of Hotel Company during the withdrawal to LZ Blue.

2/4. 1400

Bull Fisher was very concerned about Hotel Company. He had good communications with Golf and Echo, and with the rearguard back at Chulai, but very little with 1stLt Mike Jenkins and his men. There was so much administrative traffic jamming the radio nets that it was hard to pass information to Hotel and back.

Echo Company, 2/4, was still fighting its way through the hedgerows against limited resistance. Moving just behind them with the 2/4 CP group, Gunny Ed Garr picked up several bags of shucked corn and told the troops to take handfuls and put it in their pockets. Things were moving so fast that he wasn't sure they would have time for chow. The men put a few of the kernels in their mouths and sucked on them. This helped slake their thirst in the intense heat and also softened the corn so it could be chewed and swallowed.

Echo Company finally reached its objective and dug in early in the afternoon. The 2/4 command group had air on station constantly and artillery on call all trying to help the struggling Hotel Company.

THE AMBUSH OF COLUMN 21

The BLT 3/3 rear command post set up near the RLT-7 headquarters to handle the battalion's logistics and medical needs. All the armor was ashore, a total of nine M48 gun tanks, 4 flame tanks, and eight Ontos. There was also a company of amtracs loaded with supplies. BLT 3/3 asked for two of the flame tanks and the loaded amtracs to go forward to resupply India Company, 3/3.

An amtrac platoon commanded by Lt Bob Cochran had helped bring India Company ashore in the initial assault. Cochran then received orders to return to the ship, load up on ammo and water, and swim these amtracs once again to the beach to await instructions. By the time these amtracs arrived back on shore, the infantry units were approximately a thousand meters inland.

Following a thirty-minute wait on the beach, the amtracs were ordered inland to the RLT-7 command post. Lieutenant Cochran and his twenty-three men were told that they would make a resupply run to India Company, 3/3, which was a few hundred yards farther inland.

Lieutenant Cochran rode the lead tank as the column moved out shortly after noon. Major Andy Comer, the 3/3 XO, briefed the convoy on its mission and present location. The destination and route were marked on the map and Cochran was told to follow the same route as the gun tanks, which had left a couple of hours earlier to support Hotel Company, 2/4.

The column had traveled only about four hundred meters north and west of the CP when it was hit with small arms fire from the left flank. The whole column stopped to locate the source of the firing and return fire. After a few minutes the shooting stopped and the Marines proceeded down the road to look for India Company. A few hundred meters along they reached a place where they needed to make a sharp turn. As the lead tank and the first two amtracs slowed to make the curve and enter a wooded area, the rest of the column was forced to stop. The enemy was waiting, just fifty meters away.

The platoon sergeant, SSgt Jack Marino, was riding in the rear hatch of the last tractor. He assumed they had reached their objective and, after waiting a few moments, decided to leave his vehicle and go up to speak with Lieutenant Cochran. As Marino exited his amtrac there was a loud explosion in the vicinity of the lead tank. Almost simultaneously a barrage of mortars and anti-armor fire, including 57mm recoilless rifles and RPGs, struck the amtracs.

Lieutenant Cochran had also left his vehicle for a few moments to check his column when the attack came. As the fire poured into the convoy, the lieutenant ignored it as best he could and moved from tractor to tractor to find one that had communications with the regimental command post.

The VC had selected the site well. There was little room for the Marines to maneuver. One side of the road was bordered by a rice paddy and the other side was hemmed in by a hedgerow and a dense thicket.

Cochran and Marino moved through the defenders to disperse them into defensive positions as best they could. Marino's tractor moved to face the area the fire was coming from. Dust and smoke obscured the scene. When it cleared, Marino saw that several of the amtracs had been badly hit and abandoned by their crews. Some of the crewmen took up positions in the rice paddies.

The attack forced Sgt Robert F. Batson to exit his amtrac armed only with his combat knife. When the vehicle was hit, his rifle was irretrievably pinned behind the vehicle's cargo. He was immediately cut down by enemy fire as he dashed from the disabled tractor. When they found his body the next day, he was still clutching his knife.

Among the amtracs that were badly damaged was the one from which the platoon leader was trying to gain communications. Lieutenant Cochran calmly evacuated the vehicle and insured that the machine-gun ammunition was removed to deny it to the enemy. Continuing to disregard the intense fire, he directed his men to shift to two of the other tractors. After determining that his Marines were safe, he chose the tractor with the best view of the battlefield and moved toward it. His courage was costly and he was badly hit. Unwilling to expose the men inside to further danger by having them drop the ramp, he tried to get through the crew hatch of Sergeant Marino's tractor, but he was killed as he reached it. For his extraordinary courage in the face of enemy fire, he was later posthumously awarded the Navy Cross Medal.

The Marines in the tractor next to Marino's had just brought their machine gun into action when the vehicle was hit by a RPG that glanced off the bow and hit the machine-gun turret, jamming the gun. The crew scooped up their personal weapons and abandoned the tractor. As they left, a mortar round hit the rear hatch and killed Pfc

James Kalil. Sergeant Chester Wauters took to the paddies, where he stumbled over the body of a supply sergeant who had been shot off one of the tractors and then run over and cut in half by the treads. Wauters was shot in both legs as he tried to move back to one of the occupied tractors. The crew dragged him through the emergency hatch and he spent the rest of the night loading ammunition magazines for the able-bodied.

Inside one of the vehicles a Marine said, "We're Marines, let's go get 'em!" He started out the hatch but was immediately shot through the head and killed.

The only vehicle-mounted automatic weapons returning the enemy fire were from Marino's amtrac and the lead tank, which was firing its .50-caliber machine gun at the enemy across a peanut field. Marino could not move his vehicle. As he tried, an 82mm mortar round damaged the engine, blew him out of the commander's seat, and knocked him unconscious for a few seconds.

The Viet Cong infantry, under the command of Sgt Ho Cong Tham, were closing. Although excellently camouflaged, they could be seen through the smoke and haze, as they formed into groups in every direction, waiting for the barrage to lift.

VC 57mm recoilless rifles and mortars continued to pour it on. The lead tank's .50-caliber machine gun was temporarily put out of action by a mortar round that fractured the turret. It no sooner resumed firing than a 57mm round hit the side of the turret, destroying its periscope and severely wounding two crewmen inside. The third tanker tried to depress the muzzle of the flame gun on a group of about sixty VC. He was able to traverse the turret but not depress the gun sufficiently. He fired anyway, but a bad napalm mixture prevented a full burst from the tank. What fire did come out shocked and temporarily stopped the VC, some of whom were seen trying to beat out the flames on their uniforms. Their experience may have been daunting, but there was no real damage done. The next recoilless rifle round that hit the tank killed the gunner. With this, Marino's vehicle was the only one capable of firing its automatic weapon at the enemy.

Sergeant James Mulloy was in one of the tractors when it was hit and several of his fellow Marines were wounded. Mulloy calmly tended the wounded and directed the activities of the Marines around him. His casual demeanor had a remarkable effect on restoring some sort of order out of the chaos in his immediate vicinity. With his tractor bogged down he realized it was vulnerable to being overrun because of limited visibility. He exited the vehicle he and charged through VC fire to a position in a nearby rice paddy from which he could keep the column in view. Time after time he picked off individuals and small groups of VC who massed for an assault on the column. When the VC realized that Mulloy was a major obstacle to their complete annihilation of the Marine force, they attempted to take him out of play.

Adding immensely to the confusion, one of the amtrac radio operators panicked and depressed the call button on his radio for over an hour while he pleaded nonstop for help. This essentially jammed the amtrac radio network and prevented the RLT CP from receiving accurate information about the column. Lieutenant Dave Steel was the one who got the cries for help from the young Marine.

As soon as the regimental CP learned of the ambush it began putting together a rescue operation. As the afternoon, and then the night, dragged on, Lt Steel talked to the frightened Marine in the command tractor. The VC had his tractor surrounded, the lad reported, and kept shooting into the side of it and putting grenades against the cupola in attempt to blow it open and finish off the occupants. Everyone in that tractor was dead except for him.

INDIA COMPANY, 3/3

Just about the time India Company was ready to move out to rejoin the battalion main body, a Huey helicopter from VMO-2 was damaged by ground fire and had to land near the company position. When this was reported to LtCol Joe Muir, he instructed Lt Richard Purnell to leave two squads and the tanks behind to protect the helicopter. The small detachment could move out on the double and catch up with the rest of the company when the helicopter was repaired.

The helicopter did not seem to be badly damaged. The fuel tanks had been pierced, but the pilot said he could fix the problem and be out of there within half an hour. Purnell didn't *have* two squads to leave behind, certainly not two full-strength squads. He left ten Marines and the tanks. The remainder of the diminished infantry company moved to rejoin the battalion. The ten Marines and the tanks set up a perimeter around the helicopter and waited. After the bird was repaired, it dropped its rocket pods to lighten the load, and took off.

Just as the guard detachment was preparing to depart, Chris Cooney's 1st Platoon of Hotel, 2/4, which had been cut off from its parent company, found the little group guarding the downed helicopter. Cooney's Marines, who were carrying their dead and wounded, and had no working radio, were relieved to find other Marines. The engineers attached to the platoon helped the India Company Marines blow the helicopter rocket pods to prevent the explosives from being used by the enemy.

The march to rejoin the remainder of India Company was marred by repeated contact with the enemy. The small force had to change its route several times in order to move around the points of contact. Burdened with their casualties, these Marines nevertheless hustled to catch up with the rest of India Company and move on to the battalion position about sixteen hundred meters northeast of An Cuong 2. India Company finally moved into the battalion's main line abreast of Kilo Company a little after noon.

COLUMN 21. 1300. RESCUE ATTEMPT

No one realized until much later that the fight between the supply column and the VC might have saved the RLT-7 command post from being overrun. It seemed likely that that is where the VC force was headed when it ran into the convoy. The enemy survivors have since denied this with the explanation that they did not know where the command post was. Major Andy Comer also thought that the VC seemed to have very good intelligence and flexibility, and he assumed that they had monitored the Marine radio frequencies, which turned out to be true. The Viet Cong employed a great number of college and high school students who had studied English to intercept and translate American radio traffic. Marine communications security was no better than their camouflage discipline, which is to say they had very little to none.

Just before 1300, when word of the ambush reached the headquarters, Joe Muir decided to recycle India Company back into the fight. No one knows why Muir sent his most battle-weary company back to the rescue of Column 21. Marines' Marine that he was, Muir undoubtedly had sound reasons. He most likely assessed the capabilities of all of his companies and committed the one that had the best knowledge of the battlefield. Whatever the reason, his decision was a good one.

Lima Company was switched to the position formerly held by India, thus placing Kilo and Lima abreast in original line of the assault. The battalion was now without a reserve.

Before India could go to the rescue of the supply column, it had to go back to the RLT supply area and pick up some amtracs, tanks, and Maj Andy Comer, who was to lead the rescue. A group of five amtracs and five Ontos was designated to support the mission. Also, Colonel Peatross committed his last available gun tank to the rescue. The plan was for a fast-moving armored-infantry column to take the VC by surprise and quickly break through to the supply column.

The exact location of the besieged column was unknown. About the time the rescue force was to depart, one of the ambushed flame tanks roared into the CP. This tank's .50- caliber machine gun was out of action, its periscope was destroyed, two of the crew were wounded, and its .30-caliber was out of ammunition. Despite all he had been through, the flame tank commander volunteered to lead the rescue force to the site of the ambush. He noted that he had passed through An Cuong 2 without incident.

Lieutenant Purnell's India Company Marines boarded the vehicles. Some of the infantrymen rode inside the vehicles and others, because of the intense heat, and the fact that the tractors carried 500 gallons of gasoline in cells beneath the troop compartment, opted to ride on top.

The rescue column started out at 1305. A few hundred meters and a few minutes away, as they passed over a heavily wooded hill east of An Cuong 2, the lead tank was hit in the front by an RPG. When the tank stopped, the column jammed up in a rapid halt and began to receive mortar and small arms fire.

The tractor on which Pfc Howard Miller was riding was rocked with a hit, and most of the Marines riding on the top were thrown to the ground. Miller was tossed in the direction of the fire. He could hear people screaming inside the tractor as the vehicle crew tried to get the ramp down. The tractor rocked back and forth, but the ramp could be lowered only about a third of the way.

Sergeant Peter Towne was critically wounded and remained under very heavy fire. Another Marine tried to drag Towne to cover but Sergeant Towne died.

When the attack began Pfc Gary Hammett rolled off his tractor to the right. He no sooner had than a mortar round landed just to his rear. A Marine behind Hammett who absorbed the blast died immediately, but Hammett was spared.

Sergeant George Emerick was riding atop an amtrac when an RPG blew two other Marines off the vehicle with minor wounds and wounded two crewmen inside. Emerick was dazed and frightened but uninjured. He could not, however, find his rifle. He disembarked from the amtrac and helped tend the wounded. His rifle was found the next day, or at least a five-inch piece of the barrel and receiver group was found. The serial number identified it as his weapon.

Enemy action disabled the lead tractor, whose wounded crewmen were carried to safety in the next amtrac in line. The tank, in its haste to cover itself, rammed backward into the disabled amtrac and then maneuvered to a concealed position behind some tall trees. All attempts to communicate with the tank failed. The tank-infantry phone on the rear was smashed and the crew did not respond to radio calls.

A section of Ontos under the command of Lieutenant Malloy deployed to suppress the enemy fire and protect the rest of the column. Purnell left Lt Jack Kelly behind with one rifle platoon to handle casualties and provide security for Major Comer's group.

The VC put out a lot of fire in the direction of the medevac helicopters that answered the call to pick up the casualties. Lieutenant Paul Bronson and his copilot Lt Roger Cederholm, were in the lead aircraft. Bronson told his wing, flown by Lt Dan Armstrong and Lt R.G. Adams, to stay high while he went down. There was a Marine standing upright amongst the fire to direct the helicopter's descent. Bronson was down to about two hundred feet from the ground when a large group of VC in the hedgerows stood up and filled the helicopter full of holes. Armstrong and Adams immediately dropped low from around a thousand feet and worked over the enemy with their M60 machine guns. Bronson yelled over the radio that he had lost control of the RPM in his bird, but he leveled out and headed for the beach. He later learned that the hydraulic servo had been shot out, taking with it control over the engine RPM and the fore and aft control of the helicopter.

The beach was about a mile away, but the bird was sinking fast. The other aircraft flew wing on Bronson's port side. At the last moment the nose eased up and the stricken aircraft crashed through some sampans parked on the beach.

Bronson no sooner landed than he began taking heavy fire from a nearby hedgerow. The crew chief, Corporal Clouse, was hit in the stomach, and his intestines were spilling out. The door gunner was superficially wounded in the foot. Bronson jumped down from the flight deck, shoved Clouse's guts back in, and carried him to the other aircraft as Cederholm turned off the mags and applied the rotor brake. The door gunners in the second bird suppressed enemy fire, and then picked up Bronson's crew and evacuated them to the medical station. Clouse survived and Bronson received the Bronze Star Medal for his actions in saving him.

Major Comer and Lieutenant Purnell quickly devised a plan to continue their attack on foot. They hoped to clear An Cuong 2 and continue the search for the original convoy. This was the same area India Company had passed through several hours earlier, an area they had thought was secure. The event was easier planned than executed. The VC in their path were well dug in.

THE OVERALL SITUATION. 1500

Golf and Echo companies, 2/4, were at their assigned objectives. Golf had received only token resistance, but Echo had had a bit of a fight, which it handled well. Hotel, 2/4, had finally taken Hill 43 but had failed twice in its attempt to secure Nam Yen 3, although it had killed very many Viet Cong before it was ordered back to LZ Blue.

Kilo and Lima companies, 3/3, had driven inland several thousand meters and were poised to strike at Van Tuong 1. India Company, 3/3, had been severely battered and had lost its company commander in the taking of An Cuong 2. It was ordered back to the main battalion position and then sent back into the fight once more to try and find the isolated and besieged supply convoy.

The regimental and 3/3 command groups were about 3,000 meters inland. All of the RLT's tanks and Ontos had been committed, but the first elements of the 3d Battalion, 7th Marines, had arrived offshore.

CHAPTER 10

THE CALL FOR REINFORCEMENTS

3/7 LANDS. 1500

At about 1500, Colonel Peatross decided he needed more Marines on the ground, so he ordered the landing of the Special Landing Force, the 3d Battalion, 7th Marines (3/7), under the command of LtCol Charles H. Bodley. BLT 3/7 had been ashore in the Philippines when the call came on August 16, for it to steam toward the operations area. The troops were to remain aboard their ships unless needed in the fight, and now their time had come. One company, Lima, was trained as the battalion's heliborne assault company, and it was aboard the USS *Iwo Jima,* a helicopter-landing carrier, as was India Company. The fastest of the ships in its group, the *Iwo* arrived on the scene hours ahead of the slower troopships bearing the rest of BLT 3/7.

BLT 3/7 had had some brief experience in Vietnam. Supported by helicopters from LtCol Norman Ewers's HMM-163, the battalion had landed earlier at Qui Non to provide security for U.S. Army units that were being transferred into the country as part of the American buildup.

En route up the coast toward the Starlite area on August 18, the 3/7 Marines figured that something important was about to happen. Although the junior men weren't told much, the officers had an unusual number of meetings at night. And as they approached Vietnam, the food got better. The oldtimers in the group thought this was a sure sign of impending combat. Shipboard life was a lot softer than life ashore. Exercise room was limited, some of the troop spaces were air-conditioned, and the food was relatively good. All throughout the Vietnam War units that spent any considerable time aboard ship as the Special Landing Force came ashore a little softer than when they went aboard. BLT 3/7 was no exception.

The coastline of Vietnam came into view on the afternoon of August 18. The Marines aboard the *Iwo Jima* described the sight as like going to a war movie. Before their very eyes, aircraft were dropping bombs and napalm, and ships were firing naval gunfire support. Most of the troops had been through the landing drill dozens of times, but this time it would be for real.

The call came over the intercom for all Marines to report to their compartments. Captain Ron Clark, the Lima Company commander, came into his company's berthing spaces looking grim. He told the gathered Marines that the units ashore had really stepped in it and needed help. The Lima, 3/7, Marines formed into their helo teams and moved to the hangar deck, where they lined up to draw stuff that they were never allowed to touch except on the firing range: fragmentation and smoke grenades, and extra magazines that they loaded with live ammo.

Corporal Bob Collins, a fire team leader, was standing with his helo team when Cpl C. C. Pearch walked up, gave him a hug, and said, "God bless you, boy." Pearch was a veteran with eighteen years' service. He had been in the famed Chosin Reservoir march in Korea in 1950, but he was a corporal now because he had been courtmartialed and reduced in rank while serving as a drill instructor. He had two Purple Heart Medals for wounds received in Korea. Pearch's attempt to comfort Collins had the opposite effect. Collins didn't have to be there. His enlistment had been due to expire the previous June, before 3/7 had deployed for Vietnam. He had not wanted to miss out on the excitement, so he voluntarily extended his enlistment to go to war. On August 18, 1965, he was beginning to question the wisdom of his decision.

As the Marines finished their preparations, the call came for stretcher bearers to lay up to the flight deck to receive casualties. When the elevator came back down to the hangar deck, it was crammed with wounded. One was a South Vietnamese Popular Forces soldier. As his stretcher passed Collins, the man's boot fell off onto the deck. When Collins picked up the boot, he discovered there was a foot inside it. The Vietnamese grimaced and said, "It's okay, Joe, it's okay," as they bore him off to the operating room.

The 3/7 helicopter teams were cut down in size because the heat and humidity reduced lift, and the Marines were lightly burdened. Although the troops wore helmets, they did not wear flak jackets, and each carried only a light marching pack with no blanket roll.

As a helo team commander, Corporal Collins's job was to count off his men as they boarded, and to be the last one on. He would ride in the door of the chopper and be the first one off, showing his men where to fan out and secure the landing zone. This exercise had been practiced many times. Lima Company's 2d Platoon, to which Collins belonged, was always the first one in to secure the zone. His team would secure the twelve o'clock sector of the zone while the second and third teams secured the four- and eight-o'clock positions.

*   *   *

Lima, 3/7, landed without incident at 1543 in the vicinity of Colonel Peatross's command post and was immediately attached to 3/3 with the mission of advancing to the area in which India Company, 3/3, was still engaged with the enemy. Lieutenant Colonel Joe Muir ordered Lima, 3/7, to help India Company, 3/3, find the missing supply column.

The company moved out in the direction of An Cuong 2 and almost immediately received sporadic sniper fire. As the Marines returned fire tracers from their machine guns set some of the hedgerows on fire, adding smoke, confusion, and more heat to the chaotic situation. A flame tank parked near the command post rolled over and sprayed the area with its .50-caliber cupola gun. The VC fired again and were rewarded by a burst of napalm from the tank's main gun.

Once the entire company was ashore, the 2d and 3d platoons moved out in the direction from which the VC fire had come while the 1st Platoon remained behind for security.

The Marines had just started forward when Cpl Bob Collins passed what he thought was a black glove. When he picked it up bones fell out; he realized he had just picked up a human hand.

Private First Class Jim "Guts" Guterba was amazed that for all the dangerous activity around him, the flies and dragonflies carried on as if there was no war at all. When he felt the first enemy rifle bullet go by his ear his legs went numb and he dropped to his knees and hyperventilated. Someone tugged at his belt and a voice said, "Get up, kid, you're not hit yet." It was Sergeant Stone, another of Lima, 3/7's, Korean War vets. Guterba noticed that when the advance was halted by enemy fire some of the more experienced old hands rolled over on their backs and ate a C-ration. "Hey, you gotta eat 'em when you can," was the explanation. This was not only practical advice, it had a calming effect on the younger Marines.

Evidence of previous fighting was everywhere. They came across a place where marks of tracked vehicles were clearly impressed into the ground. A blackened, swollen body, split open like a hot dog ruined on the grill, lay nearby. Maggots had already claimed it, and the stench was powerful. This was quite a shock to those Marines of Lima Company whose only association with death was a body in peaceful repose in a funeral home.

Water ran short early on, but the Lima, 3/7, Marines were warned to not drink from the village wells or rice paddies. The men in 2/4 and 3/3 had learned that halizone tablets caused the water to taste terrible, but at least it made the water safe to drink. The Marines carried their water, moreover, in the old-style metal canteens that heated it up to the point where it was barely palatable in a tropic climate. The Marines from 3/7 paid the tariff for their softer life aboard ship as they began taking heat casualties.

As Lima, 3/7, advanced, the troops collected prisoners and VC suspects. Some of the enemy gave up readily, but others tried to give the impression that they were villagers. In due course, all men of military age were rounded up, tied together with communications wire, and marched to the rear. Jim Guterba was escorting one VC and a Marine ahead of him was escorting another when they took fire from their right flank. Dirt flew as bullets hit the deck, and both Marines leaped over a paddy dike. A prisoner went down and Guterba ran back to find the man lying in the hot dirt, gasping. He had a gaping thigh wound. The thighbone glistened brightly in the sunlight through the torn muscle. Guterba jammed his own battle dressing into the man's wound, only to be admonished by one of the older vets: "Better keep that for yourself, son." Guterba hoisted the man to his shoulder and continued on to the prisoner collection point. When the VC gestured that he wanted to be let down. Guterba lowered him to the ground. The man stuck one leg out and, while crying, shivering, and weeping in pain, defecated. When the man finished, Guterba once more hoisted him up and finished the journey to the collection point.

When Lima Company, 3/7, arrived at its objective area at about 1845, it was immediately welcomed by VC mortars, automatic weapons, and small arms. A Marine flame tank silenced some of the resistance when it spat napalm in the direction of the fire, but the stench of corpses rotting in the intense tropical heat and burned flesh became nearly unbearable.

Enemy mortars burst among the Marines with terrible effect. As they hugged a paddy dike, word was passed down the line. Wilson was dead, Long was dead, Firth was dead. Lieutenant Dale Shambaugh, the 3d Platoon commander, had been shot and killed by a sniper. Lance Corporal Gregorio Valdez, Cpl Bob Collins's automatic rifleman, took a hit through the ankle. Collins, kept yelling for him to move up to the dike and fire his weapon at a machine gun that was giving them a lot of trouble. "Get moving!" Collins shouted. "You can't be scared at a time like this." "I'm hit, not scared," came the reply. Wondering why Valdez hadn't said so in the first place, Collins and another Marine, LCpl Robert Parker, scrunched forward to retrieve him. They were able to do so safely because the enemy gunner could not depress his gun far enough to hit them without exposing his own position. Greg Valdez was rescued and survived Operation Starlite, but he died in another battle five months later.

The Marines discovered that some of the most macho among them in peacetime became very careful when real bullets were being fired, and that some of those most reticent around the barracks were tigers in combat. One man in the latter category charged over a dike alone and opened fire with his automatic rifle. By the time his comrades caught up with him there were four VC bodies lying in front of him. The fire had disemboweled one of the Viet Cong, whose intestines glittered in the sunlight.

A mortar round practically landed on Pfc C. B. Hitt, an assistant automatic rifleman, and tossed him into the air. Hitt was physically uninjured, but he lay stiff as a board until the shock wore off.

Private First Class L. M. Grant, an M79 man, was hit. Lance Corporal Don Parker was wounded in the arm and couldn't hold his rifle, so as he crawled past Grant he took the latter's .45 pistol and continued to move toward the enemy with that.

It was getting dark, but VMO-2 Hueys continued to pour fire into the bank ahead of the Marines.

Bob Collins felt a sting in his side and thought he must have been hit. A hurried investigation revealed that he was laying on one of his own grenades, which was digging painfully into his side. He realized the grenade might be the solution to the machine gun that was firing at them. As Collins approached the machine gun bunker, one of the VC jumped up and emptied a magazine in his direction, reloaded, and continued to fire. Collins hesitated as he had yet to kill a man in combat. Lance Corporal Larry Falls, an automatic rifleman, came up from behind Collins and cut the enemy soldier in half with a full magazine of bullets. Collins finally threw the grenade. After the explosion the enemy scattered, some of them in the direction of the Marines, who killed them as they ran by. An estimated sixteen VC were killed in this exchange of fire, but only five bodies were actually counted.

Another VC shot a carbine at one of the Marine lieutenants. A machine gunner, LCpl Charlie Davis, tried to kill him, but his gun jammed. Reacting quickly, Davis dropped the gun, pulled out his .45, and shot the man with that. He was later awarded the Vietnamese Cross of Gallantry. Davis's weapon was not the only one to misfire that day. Guterba's did, too, when he tried to fire on some VC who were running away. By the time he got the weapon cleared, the VC were gone.

Corporal Collins rolled over to a corner of a field and found a trench and dike. As he and other Marines moved up the trench they encountered a VC about twenty feet away. As the enemy soldier turned to run, Collins pumped three shots into him.

Collins and a Marine named Clark paused in the gathering darkness to watch an amtrac burn in a field to their left front. As they hugged the deck and peered down a trail a voice asked them, "What are you doing, pressing your buttons?" It was LtCol Joe Muir, the 3/3 CO, who was checking on the situation. Collins replied, "Yes, sir, I'm getting as close to Mother Nature as I can." The colonel laughed and moved on.

*   *   *

Joe Muir was a leader who repeatedly exposed himself to danger with the assault companies and personally supervised as much of the battle as he could. General Walt gently chided him for repeatedly positioning himself at the scene of the most violent action, and during Starlite he went without sleep for nearly three entire days. He was a hero on Starlite, but he died when he stepped on a booby-trapped 155mm shell just three weeks after this action, the first Marine battalion commander killed action in Vietnam. He was posthumously awarded the Navy Cross Medal for Starlite.

*   *   *

On his last flight of the day, HMM-361's Maj Al Bloom responded to yet another colored smoke grenade signaling a medevac. Bloom picked up the severely wounded casualty and was lifting out of the LZ when Master Sergeant Hooven informed him that the H-34 had been hit in the tail rotor drive shaft. The shaft was a thin, hollow tube that ran the interior length of the helicopter and was open and visible in the cargo compartment. Without the shaft, the tail rotor would be lost and the bird would spin uncontrollably and violently around its vertical axis until it crashed. As he checked his controls and saw that he still had command of the aircraft, Bloom was told by Hooven that the tube was still rotating and not vibrating in its brackets, Bloom made the decision to take the helicopter home.

After shutting down in Danang, Bloom's fighter-pilot second seat, Maj Homer Jones, pronounced all helicopter pilots crazy and vowed never to fly with them again.

With wide-eyed wonder, and a great deal of appreciation for Sikorsky, the manufacturer of the H-34, the crew inspected the damage to their bird. There were at least a dozen unauthorized holes in the skin of the ship in addition to the one that had carried away about a third of the circumference of the tail rotor drive shaft. Master Sergeant Hooven later told Bloom that he heard no more criticism about "airedales" from 1st Sergeant Dorsett, who was undoubtedly regaling his comrades in the infantry community about his aerial combat experience.

Back at Danang the number of flyable HMM-361 helicopters continued to drop. By late afternoon the squadron had eight that could not fly at all despite the heroic efforts of ground crews to get them back in the air. One on the beach was so badly damaged that it was declared unrepairable and an air strike was called on it to keep its guns and ammunition from falling into enemy hands. To HMM-361's great relief, LtCol Norm Ewers's HMM-163 H-34s took over some of the medevacs business and other critical duties after it had dropped Lima, 3/7, ashore. HMM-163 had served ashore in Vietnam for more than four months before it was assigned to the Special Landing Force. It was, by the standards of the day, very experienced in Vietnam operations. The squadron flew 232 sorties on August 18, and a total of nearly three thousand sorties over the next week, during which it medevaced 197 Marines.

* * *

As the afternoon lengthened, Lt Dave Steel needed to get to Lieutenant Colonel Muir's position. He ran into Colonel Peatross, who offered Steel a ride on his helicopter. He went along and hopped off the bird with Peatross when the colonel stopped to check with 2/4. Peatross walked up to Fisher and said, "Hey, Bull, how are you doing?" The ever-expressive Bull Fisher turned to face Peatross and said something like, "Goddammit! Fuck! I need water! Water! You understand me? I put in for fuckin' water for my people and I need fuckin' water!" The unflappable Peatross reached around to remove his canteen from its case and handed it to Fisher. Fisher flung it to the ground and yelled, "I don't mean for me, goddammit. I want fuckin' water for my fuckin' troops. I want water, and I want it now!" Pausing for breath for a moment, Fisher noticed Lieutenant Steel and said, "Oh, hi, Dave," and then returned to his tirade about water. Peatross immediately got on the radio to do what he could to get water to the troops.

* * *

As darkness fell enemy fire prevented the lead elements of 3/7 from getting to the disabled amtracs, but they thought they might be able to close on a knocked-out tank. A lieutenant came up to ask Cpl Bob Collins to select two volunteers to go across a field to check the tank for survivors. Neither Collins nor the lieutenant wanted to pick anyone else, so the two scurried across to have a look. The crew had been evacuated, but there were body parts and several rifles lying about.

While Collins was still up on the tank, some firing close by startled him. Sergeant Bill Stone loomed out of the dark and explained that he had shot a dog that was pulling on a body. Stone was another oldtimer—he had sixteen years in the Corps—who went over the wall at Inchon during the Korean War. When Collins got down from the disabled vehicle, he gathered up the rifles, removed their ammunition, put their bolts in his pack, and bent the barrels in the tank tracks to render them useless. After they returned to their position someone approached from behind them. A challenge was issued but the apparition did not answer so the Marines opened up.

*   *   *

Lima Company, 3/7, saddled up for a scary night march that took it back to the 3/3 perimeter. The only way the troops could stay together was to hold onto the belt of the men in front of them. An ambush by the enemy would have had terrible effect.

HOTEL, 2/4. 1630

The remainder of Hotel, 2/4, had completed its movement back to LZ Blue at 1630. Another air strike was made on Hill 43 to insure that no VC were still up there. Hotel Company was instructed by Bull Fisher to set in at LZ Blue in a night defensive position. These weary Marines were still getting sporadic small arms fire from Nam Yen 3, so the Ontos and tanks proceeded to level all the houses that remained standing, which helped eliminate the small-arms threat.

Exhausted from a long day of combat, Lt Mike Jenkins told his twenty-four infantry Marines, three tank crews, and three Ontos crews that they needed to dig in for the night in the strongest possible defense. When Lieutenant Jack Sullivan asked Jenkins what John Wayne would have done in a situation like this, Jenkins immediately replied, "Circle the wagons." And that they did. The tracked vehicles formed a circle, the operational ones towing the disabled ones, and the infantry Marines dug in around and beneath them. At 1800 these Marines were resupplied with food, water, and ammo. They requested fuel for the Ontos, which were down to one-eighth tank each and thus unable to travel any distance. They also were reinforced with an 81mm mortar section. Private First Class Jim Mazy, who had the only working radio, was pretty busy receiving and sending messages to Colonel Fisher's CP throughout the long night. The enemy left them alone and they spent a fairly quiet but extremely nervous night. The jittery Marines fired whenever they thought they saw something in the spooky light of the illumination flares.

CHAPTER 11

THE SITUATION AT LATE AFTERNOON

By late afternoon the Marines had effectively encircled the objective area. The coastline (see map) runs from northwest to southeast. The northwest was blocked by Mike Company, 3/3, and Golf Company, 2/4. Echo Company, 2/4 stood fast in the west; Hotel Company, 2/4, was struggling to control its sector in the southwest; and India and Kilo companies, 3/3 and Lima Company, 3/7, were sweepng the area from the southeast. The fiercest fighting of the day had taken place in a few thousand square meters around the villages of An Cuong 2 and Nam Yen 3 and the ambushed supply column that lay between the two.

A Dog Named Combat

Toward the end of the day, during a lull in the fighting, a Kilo, 3/3, Marine found a tiny emaciated puppy in one of the villages. As would many American boys, he scooped the little guy up and carried him along. Later that night when he went out on a listening post he gave the pup to LCpl Ed Nicholls, who cared for him for months afterward. Combat, as he was called, became a real Marine's dog, growing fat on

C-rations and generally behaving as friendly dogs do. Articles about Combat appeared in newspapers throughout the United States, and he frequently received fan mail from school children. Combat went through several masters as they rotated out of country at the end of their tours and, eventually, he died a Marine's death; he was killed by a booby trap placed by the enemy.

India Company, 3/3. Late Afternoon

India Company, 3/3, continued its search for the supply column. As it approached An Cuong 2, the company halted when it was fired on and called in an air strike. Marine jets dropped several 250-pound bombs on the target area. The VC in the village were either killed, or had fled, and there was no more firing. West of the village were fields bordered with the ubiquitous hedgerows. They were not the usual rice fields; potatoes or something else was growing in them.

Except for the platoon that was still back with Major Comer, India Company was 2,000 to 2,500 meters from the rest of the battalion. It still had not located the supply column.

India Company pushed eight hundred meters or more past An Cuong 2 village as it got dark. When Lt Richard Purnell radioed back a request for instructions, he was told to return to the battalion position. India Company, 3/3, never did find out where the supply train was that night.

The Marines decided to light up the area with illumination rounds from artillery and naval gunfire throughout the night. While this would make it more difficult for the VC to withdraw and easier for the supply column to defend itself, it also made it hard on India Company, 3/3. On its return to the 3/3 CP area the troops had to hit the deck every few steps and wait for the parachutes from which the illumination rounds were suspended to sway slowly to earth. Otherwise they would have become well-lighted targets for the VC still active in the area.

India Company, 3/3, was about halfway back when once again it took fire, now from five or six VC in a hedgerow. The VC were just twenty-five or thirty meters away, but the India Marines were on the deck, avoiding the light from illumination rounds. One Marine was killed and another was wounded. The Marines moved reflexively into a flanking movement and poured a flood of return fire at the enemy.

When the firing ceased, one platoon checked out the hedgerow but found nothing.

At another pause along the long march, Purnell's rear-guard machine gunner spotted five VC with weapons who were carrying one of their wounded. The Marine lay alongside the trail, well concealed by the bushes, and the VC would step on him if he did not act. He got them in his sights, opened fire, and killed them all. A little after that the Marine point man, who was moving down a trenchline, came around a bend and ran face-to-face with a VC, whom he killed.

Lieutenant Purnell asked for an emergency medevac for the wounded and dead. Major Comer got in contact with a helicopter whose pilot said he would come down if it was a real emergency. It was. The pilot then asked if there was any way India Company could show him where it was. The only night signal devices available were flashlights. When the Marines on the ground said they would turn one on, the pilot reported seeing flashlights all over the place. The Marines were certain that the VC were monitoring their radio transmissions.

They finally got a blanket, covered up the flashlight, pointed it up, and blinked it on and off. The helicopter came right down. It was a much admired bit of flying; the pilot came right in with no lights at all and dropped right into the zone. The H-34 was quickly loaded and lifted off with the wounded, a dead Marine, and a man with severe asthma.

Between the fire fights, the helicopter evacuation, and the dangerous illumination, it took India Company just about all night to reach its objective. The unit got back to the battalion at approximately 0430.

3/3 AT DUSK

Colonel Peatross visited the 3/3 commander, LtCol Joe Muir, around sundown. After he left, Muir turned his two remaining companies a bit further north to a good night defensive position. He found a hill that he wanted to set in on but was determined to make sure it was free of VC before he moved on it. As Muir looked up at the hill, he said, "I'm not going to lose another Marine unnecessarily," and put on one of the finest exhibitions of calling in combat arms that Lt Dave Steel ever saw. Muir continuously raked the hill with artillery, air, naval gunfire, and his mortars. Steel simply marveled at what Muir could do with supporting arms, either simultaneously or in sequence.

The 3/3 main body had just started its advance when Lima Company, 3/7, called to request water and advise Muir that it couldn't move. Muir turned to Capt Dave Ramsey, the 3/3 S3, and said, "I am going over there". By the time he got to Lima, 3/7, too many heat-casualty medevacs, including that of the company commander, were taking place.

In the struggle to get up the hill, Dave Steel lost his college ring when it slipped off his finger. He saw it roll down the hill, paused for a moment, looked up at the top of the hill, said, "Fuck it," and continued on up the hill.

When 3/3 reached the top and set in, Lima Company, 3/7, was still at the bottom of the hill. It was nearly dark, so the leader of the platoon of India Company that was not with Purnell, SSgt Bill Wright, went down and guided the 3/7 company to the top of the hill.

Just as it got dark, an amtrac appeared out of nowhere. It was Staff Sergeant Bradley, who had simply boarded a supply amtrac on the beach and wandered around until he found the battalion. He had plenty of food, water, and ammunition. Joe Muir walked over to Bradley and said, "Well, I can't get mad. But you can't leave until tomorrow." That was okay with Bradley. He was a supply sergeant, but he wanted to be with the front-line troops.

NIGHT FALLS ON THE BATTLEFIELD

Just at dusk, Kilo Company, 3/3, called in air and naval gunfire on enemy troops moving about two hundred meters to its front. One air strike resulted in several secondary explosions.

MIKE COMPANY, 3/7. MIDNIGHT

During the night Colonel Peatross brought the remainder of BLT 3/7 ashore. India, 3/7, arrived at the regimental CP at 1800 and remained there to provide additional security for the CP. Lieutenant Colonel Bodley and his command group followed shortly.

Just before midnight, Mike Company, 3/7, arrived off the coast aboard the slow USS *Talladega*. Although most of the day's fighting was over by that time, there was nevertheless a live sound and light show that was daunting to the Marines aboard ship. They lined the rails and said things like, "Man, oh man, I'm glad we're not involved in that mess." They only enjoyed their spectator role for a few minutes before their skipper got a call from Lieutenant Colonel Bodley to prepare to land by boat at midnight. Scuttlebutt said that the enemy was escaping the battlefield in small boats and someone needed to block off their escape route. So Mike, 3/7, offloaded from the *Talladega,* down the nets just like in the movies, on its way to make the first night amphibious landing of the Vietnam War. The ship's captain did not want to put his LCVPs into the water at night. He had inadequate charts and, having been told to land the boats where the "rounds were coming together," he thought it best to go with larger craft. The entire company, about two hundred-strong, climbed down into LCMs for its trip into the beach. The LCMs ran afoul of the same sandbar that had bedeviled the 3/3 command groups the previous morning and got hung up.

When one of the platoon commanders, Lt John Covert, jumped over the side of his LCM to see how deep it was, all but his momentarily floating helmet immediately disappeared from sight. Covert ditched enough of his gear to struggle to the surface and was pulled out of the water. After getting a bit closer to the beach, the boats managed to get their ramps down, and the Marines waded in.

Mike, 3/7, moved only a short distance inland before a sergeant named Tiger stepped on some soft ground that gave way under his weight and collapsed a tunnel through which several Viet Cong were trying to escape. Tiger reached down and pulled one of them out, giving the newly landed Marines their first close-hand view of a living, breathing VC.

* * *

With the arrival of his third battalion, Colonel Peatross was able to complete his plans for the next day's action. The regimental commander's concept of action remained basically the same: Squeeze the vise around the VC and drive them toward the sea. As a result of the first day's action against the VC, he readjusted the battalions' boundaries.

*   *   *

Echo Company, 2/4, about three thousand meters north of Hotel, 2/4, set out an ambush after dark and killed a VC whom, from his armament and equipment, the troops figured to be a mortar forward observer. Some ineffective incoming fire was directed at Echo Company, but other than that, all was quiet.

COLUMN 21. THE ACTION CONTINUES

The VC moved closer to the stalled resupply column. For hours it was a desperate standoff. Staff Sergeant Jack Marino and his crewmen used hand grenades, pistols, rifles, and their one machine gun. The Marines' job was made a little easier by the VC habit of bunching up in groups of ten to fifteen. But the VC kept coming.

Marino could see four or five Marines in the rice paddies, but he couldn't tell how many of them were still alive and able to fight. He had nine effectives with him, of whom most were wounded. Of the other vehicles only one had two surviving Marines aboard who were still firing. The remainder were silent.

The fight raged on. Marino estimated that a force of several hundred Viet Cong had closed in on the column. Next to Marino's tractor was an abandoned amtrac that several VC had boarded via its ramp. One of the VC emerged with a soap dish in his hand. As he turned to show it to another VC, Sergeant Mulloy shot the two of them off the ramp from his position in the paddy. Another tractor, which the VC thought was still occupied by living Marines, was hit once more with an antitank rocket. Its only passenger was dead. Marino's vehicle took a direct hit from a 57mm round that wounded him and several other Marines. Several of these men had been wounded for the second or third time.

In the tractor whose machine gun had been knocked out early in the fight, one of the survivors was killed trying to fire his rifle from the hatch. The VC also attempted to lob grenades down the open hatch of Marino's vehicle. When Marino moved to close the hatch a burst of gunfire drove him back. The Marines inside eventually managed to get the tractor buttoned up, but the interior heat soared.

After about three hours the main body of VC left, but a group of around fifty VC in a nearby wooded area was seen at 0100 the next morning.

Staff Sergeant Jack Marino tried to get evacuation choppers in to take out the wounded, but the location of the convoy had yet to be determined. The sergeant asked for air strikes, but, yet again, the airmen were hampered because of Marino's not being able to give his position coordinates. Lieutenant Colonel Lloyd Childers, commanding officer of HMM-361, had made several low-altitude passes over the area just before dark on August 18, but he had been unable to spot the convoy.

During most of the night Lt Dave Steel kept up his conversation with the lone Marine who had been crying for help. The man kept saying, "I need help. Please come help me." Steel told him to put as much stuff over himself as possible, including the bodies of his comrades. The man screamed and cried into the radio all night. Steel asked Capt Dave Ramsey, the 3/3 operations officer, if there was any chance of getting to him. Ramsey said no; it was a hard decision, but nothing could be done that night. They weren't sure of his exact location and the VC were sure to be waiting. They had no way of knowing whether there were other survivors in the column or not. The lone Marine felt that he had been deserted. Not going after him that night was one of the toughest decisions Lieutenant Colonel Muir and Captain Ramsey ever made.

CHAPTER 12

THE SECOND DAY

At 0730 on August 19, Kilo and Lima companies, 3/3, moved out in line abreast to attack toward the northeast. Lima, 3/7, was in reserve. Simultaneously, Echo and Golf, 2/4, drove eastward toward the sea to link up with 3/3. The battered Hotel, 2/4, and India Company, 3/3, withdrew to the regimental CP, and India and Mike, 3/7, moved out from the CP to extract the supply column and on the way toward the village of An Thoi 2 to establish a blocking position that would prevent the VC from slipping southward. Mike, 3/3, was ordered to hold its original blocking position further north.

Lima, 3/7, completed the sweep to the beach with little incident. Some light sniper fire, which caused no casualties, was all these troops encountered. As they looked toward the village of Van Tuong 1 they observed several VC and called an air strike. When the strike dispersed the VC, the 3d Platoon took the fleeing enemy under fire and killed an estimated nineteen of them.

THE RESCUE

The exact location of Column 21 was not determined until after sunrise on August 19. One of the 3/3 FACs, Lt Howie Schwend, requested that all aircraft operating in the area look for it, and it was found.

The 3d Battalion, 7th Marines advanced into its zone of action, the scene of August 18's fiercest fighting. There it discovered that the VC had mostly gone. These Marines moved through An Cuong 2, met no resistance, and joined up with the supply convoy.

When the young man who had pleaded on the radio all day and all night was finally rescued the next morning, he ran out of his tractor screaming and crying about having been abandoned. "They just left me there! They abandoned me!" Ironically, although the Marine was quite bitter, he became a career Marine.

The VC left a booby-trapped C-ration box on the ramp of the vehicle next to Marino's. It was discovered and disarmed by the engineers.

More than sixty enemy bodies were found in the vicinity of the column. Others undoubtedly had been hauled away.

One tractor was deemed irreparable and blown up by engineers on the spot. The wreckage remains there today, and the Vietnamese have built a war memorial around it. Of the remaining vehicles, only one could move under its own power; the remainder had to be towed by a tank retriever.

Sergeant James Mulloy, who had positioned himself in the rice paddy, thwarted the VC effort to overrun the column for hour upon hour. He inflicted an extraordinary number of casualties on the Viet Cong. When aid arrived that morning he insured that all the wounded men were evacuated before seeking relief for himself. James Mulloy was awarded the Navy Cross Medal for his heroic efforts.

Jack Marino, who received the Silver Star Medal for his actions during the fight, counted five recoilless rifle or RPG hits on his vehicle, more than three hundred fifty bullet holes, and damage from an 82mm mortar round that knocked out the engine.

3/7

Lima, 3/7, was in its blocking position by 1500. In Van Tuong 3 and Van Tuong 4, these troops apprehended eight young males of military age and turned them over to the intelligence officer for questioning.

India and Mike companies, 3/7, patrolled over the ground on which Hotel, 2/4, had fought so hard the day before. They found packs and minor pieces of equipment but nothing of great value.

2/4 AND 3/3

The main bodies of 2/4 and 3/3 encountered scattered pockets of VC on their sweep to the sea. The terrain was difficult; compartmented rice paddies ringed by dikes and hedgerows hindered observation for control purposes and hampered maneuverability. The few VC left in the area were holed up in scattered tunnels and caves. Marines moving through the area often sustained sniper fire from the rear. Blasting the tunnels and caves was slow, hot work.

Echo Company, 2/4, and the battalion command group swept through Van Tuong 1. Gunny Ed Garr thought it was one of the spookiest places he ever saw. He had both pistols out and at the ready, and he made sure he didn't get near any radio antennas on the way through the village. VC snipers' favorite targets were the radio operators and those around them, who would be correctly presumed to be members of the command group.

The hedgerows and fences channeled the foot traffic through narrow lanes, perfect for booby traps or ambushes. The Marines discovered several thousand punji stakes in a schoolyard and surmised that children had made them during school breaks. An old man helped destroy them.

Even though it was full daylight, the village had a double canopy of vegetation over it and seemed awfully dark and foreboding. As were most of the villages in the area it was honeycombed with bunkers.

The Marines picked up so many packs and so much communications wire that they were certain this had been the 1st VC Regiment command post. They were right. The commanders thought a more thorough search was in order and called the RLT-7 headquarters to recommend that an ARVN or other unit conduct a detailed search after they passed through. The march to the sea was complete and organized resistance ceased by nightfall.

WRONG WAY

Corporal Robert O'Malley's men, Buchs and Rimpson, stayed aboard the hospital ship the first night, but they decided that they were not wounded badly enough to prevent them from rejoining the fight. The rumor mill, which always works overtime during and after a big fight, had it that India Company, 3/3, had been wiped out.

The two Marines hitched a ride back to the battalion armory in Chulai, where they drew new weapons and managed to get a ride back to the ship. From there they caught an amtrac headed for the beach and rejoined the battalion. They saw no more action on Starlite as, by this time, India Company had been withdrawn to the beach to serve as command post security. Long after the battle, other troops marveled at the fact that these two had a legitimate reason to stay away from a very dangerous battlefield and had chosen to return. Although truly admired for their decision they took a lot of ribbing from the others. Rimpson, in particular, was singled out for the sobriquet "Wrong Way Rimpson."

LOOSE ENDS

General Walt continued Starlite for five more days in the hope that his troops would find more of the enemy in caves and tunnels. Fisher's and Muir's battalions were withdrawn on August 20, and LtCol James Kelly's 1/7 entered the area to work with 3/7. Troops of the 2d ARVN Division came into Starlite on the third day of the operation and policed up VC who were still operating on the fringes of the peninsula. They brought up three or four battalions along the coastline from south of Chulai to keep VC from escaping in that direction. Their efforts yielded few results. The 2d ARVN Division commander, BriGen Hoang Xuan Lam, met with Colonel Peatross on several occasions. Peatross trusted Lam completely and thought that there would be no leaks from him. Lam and some of his staff visited Peatross and the 7th

Marines during Starlite, and after that they worked very closely together.

* * *

The VC who had wanted to leave were gone. They departed the first night, exiting near where Hotel Company, 2/4, was dug in for the night and then on past an ARVN outpost to the south, where the right people were bribed to ignore their passage.

The Bo Doi claim that they broke off the battle at the end of the first day because, "we were tired, and the Americans were tired." They left one company behind under the command of Phan Tan Huan to help the villagers deal with the casualties and harass the Marines. Clashes between the two sides were generally light, and there were few casualties on the Marine side. The effort cost the VC another sixty or so killed in action. No more Marines were killed by the VC activity.

The Bo Doi said that they considered bringing in their other two battalions from the south when the battle began but rejected that idea out of fear of the effect American fire power would have on the units moving in the open during daylight.

* * *

Operation Starlite was over, but it would remain in the collective memory of the Marines for a long, long time.

CHAPTER 13

THE REACTION

By the time the rescued Marines were returned to the RLT-7 CP about twenty-five correspondents showed up to be briefed about the operation. New Zealander Peter Arnett cornered the young man who had been crying on the radio and asked him questions about events of the previous day. Then, without a word to anyone else, Arnett went off and filed a story that alleged that the Marine Corps had lost, that it had failed to rescue its people, and that the Marine leaders did not have a true grasp on the combat situation at hand on August 18.

Captain Richard Johnson, a member of the 3d Marine Division operations staff, filed a second story that differed substantially from Arnett's. He did so at the request of Col Don Wyckoff, the III Marine Amphibious Force operations officer, because so many queries came in as a result of Arnette's piece.

Captain Johnson and some other officers arrived in Saigon to brief General Westmoreland and his staff on the morning of August 21. Afterwards they were asked to brief the correspondents at the Saigon press center. In addition to Johnson the Marines were represented by Major Williamson, the 3d Marine Division intelligence officer; a squad leader from Hotel Company, 2/4; an F4 pilot; and an aerial observer, all of whom had participated in the operation. The briefing went well until Arnett, at the very end, shot his hand up and asked Johnson why he disputed his (Arnett's) version of the story. Johnson related what actually happened and pointed out that he (Johnson) had been within a few hundred meters of the incident, whereas Arnett had been nowhere near the battlefield.

Arnett shot back that Johnson was a liar and challenged him to meet him (Arnett) at the Associated Press office, where he would produce documentary evidence of what happened. Because of the exchange of words the head of the Saigon press center terminated the briefing. Johnson and the others were caught in the crush of other correspondents who approached them to ask questions, including at least one who apologized for Arnette's actions.

It took Johnson about fifteen minutes to break away and get to the Associated Press office, which they found locked. There was no sign of Arnett. They found this curious, because most press offices were open twenty-four hours a day.

Johnson never encountered Arnett again, but the reporter won the Pulitzer Prize and established his reputation with this article, whose authenticity the Marines still question.

*   *   *

"Marines Trap 2,000 VC" was one headline of many that hit front pages across the nation. It was, indeed, a promising time for America's effort in Vietnam. President Lyndon Johnson was so ecstatic he sent a message to Generals Westmoreland and Walt that said in part, "I extend my heartfelt thanks and congratulations to the units under your command which have achieved a clear cut victory against the 1st Viet Cong Regiment at Chulai. This nation is deeply proud of its fighting sons. *They will have the continued, united, and determined support of their people at home.*"

And for a while they did. The anti-war demonstrations and teach-ins had not yet begun, and they wouldn't reach a crescendo until after the Tet Offensive of early 1968. In the aftermath of Starlite optimists on Westmoreland's staff, in the administration, and in the Congress visualized American troops rooting out and killing or dispersing large numbers of enemy soldiers in a short period of time.

The Marines had passed their first big test in Vietnam. Moreover, they tested on the battlefield the combined helicopter and amphibious doctrine they had studied for more than a decade. The success of

Starlite renewed their faith in their ability to operate effectively in "any clime and place," and against any enemy.

*   *   *

Just a few weeks after Operation Starlite the Marines launched Operation Piranha against what was supposed to be the "remnants" of the 1st Viet Cong Regiment, which were thought to be on the Batangan Peninsula, about eight miles south of the Starlite battlefield.

Once again Col Peat Peatross and Navy Capt William McKinney were the commanders of the landing forces and the amphibious task force. The operation also included LtCol Charles Bodley's 3/7 and LtCol Joseph E. Muir's 3/3. This time our Vietnamese allies were included. The 2d Battalion, 4th ARVN Regiment, and the 3d VNMC Battalion were landed by helicopter in the southern portion of the battlefield. Compared to Starlite, where the planning was done instantly and the execution followed quickly, the conditions of Piranha permitted more extensive preparation. This time there was a thirteen-day interval between the time the warning order went out and the time of the landing, on September 7.

The operation was but a moderate success when compared with its predecessor. Allied forces claimed 178 VC killed and 20 weapons captured. The allies suffered two Marines and five South Vietnamese killed.[1]

The fairly low level of activity could be attributed to several factors. One difference was the fact that the Marines had a long time to plan Piranha. The extended planning phase meant a smoother operation, but it also increased the likelihood of intelligence leaks by our allies. On Starlite, only two high-ranking Vietnamese generals were notified of the operation before its execution. Because of extensive South Vietnamese participation in Pirhana, a lot of them had to know about the effort during the planning stages, which increased the likelihood of information falling into enemy hands.

Perhaps the most important reason for the so-so result was that the Viet Cong had gained an enormous appreciation of the Marines' ability to project power from the sea as a result of Starlite. Never again in the course of the war did they permit their units to tarry on the coastal plain. When they had a job to do near the water, they came in and did it, and then they fled inland again. Although they developed good antiaircraft techniques and weaponry during the war they had neither the ordnance nor the expertise to thwart an amphibious landing force.

It took a long time for American forces to gain an appreciation of the resilience of the Viet Cong. At the conclusion of Starlite the allies wrote off the 1st Viet Cong Regiment as a fighting force. A mere four months later, several Marine battalions, including 3/3, once again met the full-strength regiment near Chulai in Operation Harvest Moon. The Americans were mystified by the regiment's ability to reconstitute itself. The Marines did not know that they had encountered only half of the regiment on Operation Starlite. Nor did they have an understanding of how the VC could replenish their losses by reaching down into local guerrilla and regional force units for new men. The Ba Gia Regiment would be written off many times, but it endured throughout the war. Many thousands of Viet Cong who belonged to this unit were killed over the years, but the unit always bounced back. It was assigned as part of the 2d North Vietnamese Army Division in early 1966 and ranged back and forth between its familiar foundation in Quang Ngai Province and the Que Son Valley, to the north. At the end of Operation Swift in September 1967 the 1st VC Regiment was judged to be "unfit for combat" by allied intelligence.[2] Yet the regiment continued a vigorous program of fighting U.S. Marine and U.S. Army units and, after the withdrawal of American troops, against ARVN units.

*   *   *

The reaction to Operation Starlite among the allies was not altogether unalloyed cheer. There was grumbling to Westmoreland from ARVN officers on the Joint General Staff who resented that ARVN units had not been included. Walt later stated that Generals Lam and Thi knew of the operation and concurred with his decision to operate on a basis of secrecy.

*   *   *

The 1st VC Regiment's "Victory at Van Tuong" "demonstrated what was necessary to defeat the Americans" and the unit received the "1st Class Medal of Liberation" and the pennant of "Valor, Steadfastness, Good Combativity and Swift Destruction."[3] After the end of the war the government of Vietnam constructed memorial pavilions around the tank and amtrac that were destroyed on Operation Starlite.

Plaques in Vietnamese and English inform the visitor that they were just two of the many vehicles destroyed by the freedom fighters.

*   *   *

Starlite was a watershed for both sides. The U.S. continued to pour men and materiél into the war effort in the belief that Starlite was the beginning of a reversal of fortune in Vietnam. Ironically, Starlite, a Marine victory, reinforced General Westmoreland's notion that carrying the fight to main force enemy units was the key to success in Vietnam. This belief helped keep pacification, the Marines' focal point, in a secondary role.

For their part, the Viet Cong and the North Vietnamese Army, realized that the days of "special war" and the prospects for a quick victory had evaporated. They settled in for a long struggle. It would take them nearly a decade to achieve their aims. The Bo Doi told the author that before Starlite they feared American mobility and fire power, and were not sure how to handle with it. The operation taught them, however, that they could adapt to deal with the Americans just as they had adapted to deal with the French.

PART III

CHAPTER 14

THE BLOOD DEBT

Operation Starlite was heralded as a success throughout America's military establishment and among America's allies. The death of fifty-four Americans seemed a reasonable price for killing six hundred-some of the enemy. The operation showed that the wily and evil Viet Cong *could* be beaten with American fire power and mobility. There were Pollyanna predictions of bringing home U.S. troops soon. Few cared that in cities and towns in twenty-six states across the nations, Marine officers donned their dress blues and, accompanied by Navy chaplains, made difficult journeys to see the families of the fifty-four dead to tell them that their sons, their fathers, or their husbands had died heroically for their country. As these fifty-four families grieved their loss, fifty-four names were added to the debit side of the ledger. America's blood debt to her own people had just taken its biggest single jump to that time. Few Americans or Vietnamese realized it, but Operation Starlite was just the first outpouring of what would become a flood of corpses from Vietnam to the United States.

Fewer than than three months later U.S. Army forces entered a terrible place called the Ia Drang Valley, where they inflicted a defeat on the North Vietnamese Army. But America's debt made another quantum leap when it increased by nearly three hundred names, and three hundred more grieving families. The total liability, beginning with Major Buis and Master Sergeant Ovnand, was now 2,057.

By the end of 1965 the number would be 2,385.

Withdrawal from Vietnam, which could have been accomplished without too much furor just a few months earlier, had become an unacceptable option for the Johnson administration. How could the American President defend the expenditure of more than two thousand American lives with nothing to show for it?

Defense Secretary Robert McNamara, the numbers-driven optimist, was besieged by doubt regarding the ability of the United States to win the war militarily by "as early as late 1965 or early 1966."[1] Yet he made no real attempt to dissuade General Westmoreland from his bloody search-and- destroy strategy in favor of a pacification-driven effort combined with pressure on South Vietnam's regime du jour to genuinely reform.

The Americans would have many more "victories" the likes of Starlite, but these would be measured in terms of the notorious "body count" rather than by any measure of winning over the Vietnamese people to the concept of Western democracy.

General Westmoreland promised that sooner or later the war would reach a "crossover point," that the number of casualties inflicted on the communists would someday exceed the number of men they could replace. At this point, argued the general, the enemy forces would rapidly deteriorate in the face of continuing American and South Vietnamese victories. The crossover point proved to be ethereal; it was never reached because American planners had no real grasp of the determination of the Vietnamese people to expel foreigners from their soil. Long after the war, an American exclaimed to General Giap, "General, this war cost you over a million men." To which the general simply replied, "Yes."

America spent another ten years, and more than 56,000 additional lives, to follow a failed policy. Like gamblers who have already lost their gambling money, and then the rent money, and the car payment, and then the grocery money, and then borrowed or stole in the hope of changing their luck, the Johnson and Nixon administrations kept signing markers to America for a debt in gore that they hoped a reversal of fortune would justify.

Two months before Operation Starlite and the largest increases of American troops committed to the war, Lyndon Johnson expressed serious doubts to his intimates about whether America could win. Referring to the enemy, he told Senator Birch Bayh, "They hope they will wear us out. And I really believe they'll last longer than we do."[2]

Americans have a tolerance for loss, but only to a point. As the number of grieving families passed the 10,000 mark, and then the 15,000 mark, public protest against the war began in earnest and steadily increased.[3] By the time the blood debt hit 30,000 lives, popular opposition widened and support for the war began to melt away. The *American* crossover point had been reached, a goal the communists long kept in mind. In our case, obviously, it was not a question of losing men faster than we *could* replace them but a question of losing men faster than we were *willing* to replace them. Like the French public before it, the American public finally had enough.

Credibility with the American public was difficult to obtain when the administrations kept changing the reasons why Americans were being asked to sacrifice their sons. Hugh M. Arnold's examination of the official justification of the war found that there were a total of twenty-two separate American rationales: From 1949 to 1962, the emphasis was on resisting communist aggression; from 1962 to 1968, it was on counterinsurgency; after 1968, it was on preserving the integrity of American commitments. The Pentagon Papers have shown us that, according to McNaughton, as early 1965 70 percent of the reason was preserving the integrity of American commitments.[4] This argument might have washed in 1965, but it was unconvincing by 1968.

With no credible collateral to offer American families for their losses, the Johnson administration's position on the war became very slippery and, when the violence of the 1968 Tet Offensive horrifically added to the debt, that position became untenable. In the two-and-a-half years between Starlite and the Tet Offensive the Vietnamese communists learned how to fight the Americans. They learned to deal with American fire power in the same manner in which they dealt with that of the French. They used "grab-them-by-the-belt" tactics—that is, when engaged they moved in as close as they could to their enemy in order to negate the effects of supporting arms, which would endanger American troops when employed too close to American lines. And they quickly learned ways around our highly vaunted technical advances, one at a time. They also knew that they could never defeat the United States militarily, nor her South Vietnamese ally as long as it had American backing. As with the French, they didn't have to. Their goal was merely to *not lose* while they increased the number of coffins flowing toward America. That strategy hit dead center on America's weakest strategic underpinning, the morale of her population.

Bloodshed among the South Vietnamese climbed to enormous proportions. It is estimated by one scholar that between 1965 and 1974 there were more than 1.1 million *civilian* war casualties in South Vietnam, of which more than three hundred thousand were deaths. With a population of approximately seventeen million, this represents deaths of about 1.8 percent of the population. The same percentage applied to the United States would have resulted in approximately 3,600,000 dead. The greater number of civilian casualties were caused by the intense and impersonal weaponry of the U.S. military and the ARVN.[5] Nearly every South Vietnamese family was touched negatively by the war. It is fair to say that the Vietnamese peasant cared as little for the ideology of the North as he did for that of the South. But the VC worked on popular non-ideological support and tried very hard to pacify the people in their favor.

The U.S. military and ARVN continued to expend lives and treasure on a search-and-destroy policy that was too much search and too little destroy. So while the American government tried to explain away the blood debt to the American and Vietnamese peoples with the debased coinage of body count, the VC and NVA justified theirs to their fellow Vietnamese with the sounder currency of nationalism. It is one of the great tragedies of America and of Vietnam that American policymakers were not more familiar with Vietnam's long history of dealing with foreign invaders. America's enemy, at least after 1965, consistently and successfully portrayed the war as the result of American colonialism and painted the South Vietnamese as American puppets. Many Vietnamese who had no use for ideology of any shading found their traditional xenophobia fueled by a lengthening list of grievances over the war's death and destruction.

The Marines and Army got into it early about pacification vis-à-vis conventional warfare in Vietnam. The Marines, who had decades of experience with the former, argued passionately in favor of pacification, along with its siblings, population control and counter-insurgency. The difference was institutional. The U.S. Army of the era was trained to fight masses of Soviet tanks on the central German plain, or to resist a Korea-style invasion. U.S. Army General Samuel "Hanging Sam" Williams, one of the early progenitors of the ARVN, trained it in this fashion.[6] U.S. Army Colonel Harry Summers, in his book *On Strategy: A Critical Analysis of the Vietnam War*, describes the four pages in the U.S. Army Field Service Regulations, 1939 edition, regarding guerrilla war.[7] Four pages! The Marines had an entire book devoted to insurgency warfare, the *Small Wars Manual.*[8] Generals Krulak and Walt, and other senior officers, got their training as young officers under Marines who had fought insurrections led by Aguinaldo in the Philippines, Sandino in Nicaragua, and Charlemagne in Haiti. They understood that Vietnam was more political war than military. The U.S. Army's institutional memory on insurrection was generally confined to their 19th century campaigns against Native American tribes. General Phil Sheridan's infamous, "The only good Indian is a dead Indian" reflected the search-and-destroy philosophy of that era.

A pacification process worthy of the name with a concomitant reform within the South Vietnamese government might have saved the effort. By leaving the enemy main-force units to rot in the mountains and jungles, and by dealing with the majority of the population that resides on the coastal plain, perhaps some real political progress could have been made. Such a plan would certainly have reduced both American and Vietnamese civilian casualties and prolonged public support for the war. But Army General Westmoreland was the boss, and he had the support of the President and even an increasingly doubtful Robert McNamara. President Johnson himself had been a lukewarm supporter of pacification. The President was an impatient man, anxious to get the war won and over with. His ear was bent toward those who promised victory on the World War II model. CIA Director John McCone remarked about his first meeting with the President on the subject of Vietnam, "Johnson definitely feels that we place too much emphasis on social reforms, he has very little tolerance with our spending so much time being 'do-gooders . . . '"[9] Nonetheless, by the 1966 war conference in Honolulu, Westmoreland was told to place more emphasis on pacification. The deputy ambassador to Vietnam, William J. Porter, commented at the conference that the watchword in Washington was to be pacification."[10] Presidents Johnson of the United States and Thieu of South Vietnam issued the "Honolulu Declaration" on February 8, 1966. It restated and confirmed this policy.

Despite these words from the top, General Westmoreland did little to change his large-unit philosophy. The general nearly doubled his requirements for battalion-size operations in the coming months, which severely reduced the assets available for pacification. He told General Walt that pacification did not have universal application within Vietnam and certainly not if it was "to the detriment of our primary responsibility for destroying main force enemy units."[11] So the meat grinder operations continued and the casualty lists grew and grew until the United States was forced into a humiliating withdrawal from the country.

The noted military theorist Carl von Clausewitz wrote, ". . . even the ultimate outcome of a war is not always to be regarded as final. The defeated state often considers the outcome merely a transitory evil, for which a remedy may still be found in political conditions at some later date."[12] Will this be the case with Vietnam?

Consider the following: The West has won the Cold War, of which the Vietnam War was an important part. In the 1960s more than 60 percent of the world's population lived under governments that were, or claimed to be, communist. By 2000, except for Cuba, North Korea, Vietnam, and China, these governments are gone. Vietnam and China seem to be moving haltingly toward market economies, which can only flourish in liberal political surroundings. Cuba's government will arguably change after the passing of Fidel Castro. North Korea remains a wild card, as do several totalitarian but non-communist regimes, such as Syria, Iran, Libya, and Belorus. It is beyond the scope of this book to determine the effect that economic loss to the Soviet Union in support of their client state, Vietnam, had on its own downfall. Suffice to say that the Evil Empire is dead.

The Association of Southeast Asian Nations (ASEAN) was born behind the American bulwark in Southeast Asia in the 1960s. It has grown from five member countries in 1967 to a total of nine nations, including Vietnam, which joined in 1995. It includes such economic tigers as Indonesia, Singapore, Malaysia, and Thailand as well as struggling nations such as Vietnam and Myamar. For those nations for which data is available, per capita income is an average of two hundred thirty times higher than it was during the 1960s, and life expectancy at birth has risen from an average of fifty-six years to sixty-nine years.[13]

One of the first things that an American veteran of the war notices upon returning to Vietnam is the Pepsi Cola logo that entirely covers the shuttle buses that tourists take from the airplane to the terminal. Then there are the billboards. The first two on the way to Hanoi in 1997 were for BMW and MasterCard, hardly socialist icons. In the cities one sees signs for Hewlitt-Packard, Compaq, and Kodak. Whole city blocks are devoted to shops that sell Japanese and Korean appliances. The farmers now own land, and individuals own businesses. There are golf courses, high-rise office buildings, and luxury beach resorts. Everyone wants to be a capitalist. All the flight attendants on Vietnam Airlines speak excellent English and one other Asian language. Many Vietnamese in the cities, including small children, seem to want to say "Hello" in English. Other differences that a veteran will notice are the absences. Except for the occasional gate guards at military installations there are no armed men afoot. There is no barbed wire, no sandbags, no parachute flares at night, and no sounds of helicopters. There is scant evidence of the war even at the former American fire bases. All one can find at Con Thien, Khe Sanh, Gio Linh, and other battlefields and bases is the occasional sandbag shred sticking up from the ground and some shallow indentations where fighting holes once were. Indeed, in 1997, the author noted a farmer at Con Thien plowing with a water buffalo where the minefield had been.

Vietnam is at peace, it is unified, and is unlikely to be a threat to the region or the world. U.S. Secretary of Defense, William Cohen, returning from a trip to Vietnam, announced in March 2000 that the prospects of a military alliance between Vietnam and the United States were good.[14]

No one can tell what Vietnam's future will bring but if she moves fully into the family of nations perhaps the blood debt will finally be paid.

Epilogue

On August 18, 2000, a small group of former Marines, led by Capt Ed Garr approached the town of Chulai by bus. Buildings along the route were festooned with bunting and banners commemorating the thirty-fifth anniversary of Operation Starlite, which the Vietnamese call the Battle of Van Tuong.

Following a tour of the battlefield they gathered for lunch at a local hotel and met with former members of the Ba Gia Regiment. The conversations ranged from the battle itself, to fighting the French, to tactics used against the Americans, to how the Vietnamese identified and buried their dead. The next morning the veterans from both sides gathered at the memorial cemetery near the battlefield. The Marines presented a wreath in honor of the fallen Viet Cong as a military band played and an honor guard presented arms. There were speeches by national, provincial, and military dignitaries. At the conclusion dozens of children released hundreds of balloons into the air.

Once more, the former enemies had lunch together, shook hands all around, and then said their farewells amidst promises to meet again.

MEDAL OF HONOR CITATIONS

The President of the United States in the name of Congress takes pride in presenting the Medal of Honor posthumously to:

LANCE CORPORAL JOE C. PAUL
UNITED STATES MARINE CORPS

CITATION

For conspicuous gallantry and intrepidity at the risk of his life above and beyond the call of duty as a Fire Team Leader with Company H, Second Battalion, Fourth Marines, during Operation STARLITE near Chu Lai in the Republic of Vietnam on 18 August 1965. In violent battle, Corporal Paul's platoon sustained five casualties as it was temporarily pinned down by devastating mortar, recoilless rifle, automatic weapons and rifle fire delivered by insurgent communist (Viet Cong) forces in well-trenched positions. The wounded Marines were unable to move from their perilously exposed positions forward of the remainder of their platoon, and were suddenly subjected to a barrage of white phosphorous rifle grenades. Corporal Paul, fully aware that his tactics would almost certainly result in serious injury or death to himself, chose to disregard his own safety and boldly dashed across the fire-swept rice paddies, placed himself between his wounded comrades and the enemy, and delivered effective suppressive fire with his automatic weapon in order to divert the attack long enough to allow the casualties to be evacuated. Although critically wounded during the course of the battle, he resolutely remained in his exposed position and continued to fire his rifle until he collapsed and was evacuated. By his fortitude and gallant spirit of self-sacrifice in the face of almost certain death, he saved the lives of several of his fellow Marines. His heroic action served to inspire all who observed him and reflect the highest credit upon himself, the Marine Corps and the United States Naval Service. He gallantly gave his life in the cause of freedom.

*   *   *

The President of the United States in the name of the Congress takes pleasure in presenting the Medal of Honor to:

CORPORAL ROBERT E. O'MALLEY
UNITED STATES MARINE CORPS

For conspicuous gallantry and intrepidity in action against the communist (Viet Cong) forces at the risk of his own life above and beyond the call of duty while serving as Squad Leader in Company "I", Third Battalion, Third Marines, Third Marine Division (Reinforced), near An Cu'ong 2, South Vietnam, on 18 August 1965. While leading his squad in the assault against a strongly entrenched enemy force, his unit came under intense small arms fire. With complete disregard for his personal safety, Corporal O'Malley raced across an open rice paddy to a trench line where the enemy forces were located. Jumping into the trench, he attacked the Viet Cong with his rifle and grenades, and singly killed eight of the enemy. He then led his squad to the assistance of an adjacent Marine unit, which was suffering heaving casualties. Continuing to press forward, he reloaded his weapon and fired with telling effect into the enemy emplacement. He personally assisted in the evacuation of several wounded Marines, and again regrouping the remnants of his squad, he returned to the point of the heaviest fighting. Ordered to an evacuation point by an officer, Corporal O'Malley gathered his besieged and badly wounded squad and boldly led them under fire to a helicopter for withdrawal. Although three times wounded in this encounter, and facing imminent death from a fanatic and determined enemy, he steadfastly refused evacuation and continued to cover his squad's boarding of the helicopters while, from an exposed position, he delivered fire against the enemy until his wounded men were evacuated. Only then, with his last mission accomplished, did he permit himself to be removed from the battlefield. By his valor, leadership, and courageous efforts in behalf of his comrades, he served as an inspiration to all who observed him, and reflected the highest credit upon the Marine Corps and the United States Naval Service

GLOSSARY

105mm howitzer. The most common artillery piece used by the U.S. and the ARVN during the Vietnam War.

107mm howtar. A hybrid artillery piece consisting of a 4.2" mortar mounted on a howitzer chassis.

1st Sergeant. Pay grade E-8. The senior NCO in a company or aircraft squadron.

3.5-inch rocket launcher. Designed as a tank killer, this shoulder-fired, crew-served weapon, was commonly used as a bunker-buster in Vietnam. It fired a high-explosive antitank round or a white phosphorus round.

57mm recoilless rifle. An anti-tank weapon used by the VC and NVA.

60mm mortar. The smallest of the mortars used by the VC and NVA. Marine rifle companies also had three of these assigned to them later in the war in Vietnam.

81mm mortar. The standard general-support, organic mortar in a Marine battalion. The VC and NVA also used this mortar and the Chinese/Soviet 82mm mortar.

A4 Skyhawk. An attack aircraft used by the U.S. Marines and the U.S. Navy in Vietnam.

Adm. Admiral.

AK47. An automatic rifle used by the VC and NVA in the war, although not many were used in Starlite.

Alpha command group. The primary command group consisting of the commanding officer and key staff members.

Amphibious Squadron (Phibron). A groupment of ships in a naval task force designed to land Marines onto a hostile shore.

Amtrac. Amphibian tractor. Lightly armored tracked vehicle designed to carry troops and/or cargo from ship to beach as well as inland.

APA. Amphibious Attack transport ship. A troop ship that carried Marines to an objective area.

ARVN. The Army of the Republic of Vietnam. Pronounced to rhyme with "marvin." Our South Vietnamese allies.

AR. In the context of Operation Starlite, an M14 rifle that had been modified to fire on full automatic.

BAR. Browning Automatic Rifle. Used heavily by the United States in World War II and Korea. In the Vietnam War it was used by the VC and NVA.

Battalion Landing Team (BLT). A Marine infantry battalion with attached support units, e.g., artillery and engineer units.

Bo Doi. Literally Vietnamese for "infantry," this term has been expanded to mean something like "freedom fighter."

Bravo command group. The secondary command group of a unit. It is usually composed of the executive officer and lesser staff members.

BriGen. Brigadier general.

Bronze Star Medal. The American fourth highest decoration for valor.

Capt. Captain.

Chicom. For Chinese Communist. It referred to the type of hand grenade, made in China, that was used by the VC and NVA.

CinCPac. Commander-in-Chief, Pacific. The senior U.S. military command in the Pacific rim.

CO. Commanding officer.

Col. Colonel.

Command-detonated mine. An explosive device detonated on command by electrical means.

Commodore. An honorific denoting the senior U.S. Navy captain of a flotilla of two or more ships.

Corporal (Cpl). Third lowest Marine rank.

CP. Command Post. The field headquarters of a military unit.

C-rations. The most commonly consumed food ration of the Vietnam era.

DASC. Direct air support center. A Marine organization that controls air operations from the ground.

D-day. The day an operation begins.

F4 Phantom. A fighter/attack aircraft used by the Marines, Navy, and Air Force in the Vietnam War. It was crewed by two men.

Five-paragraph order. A combat order orally given to Marines for an operation.

Flame tank. A regular tank chassis carrying a napalm gun rather than a standard 90mm gun.

FO. Artillery or mortar forward observer.

Fragmentary order or **frag order.** An abbreviated version of the five-paragraph order.

Gen. General.

Gunny. Short for gunnery sergeant.

GySgt. Gunnery sergeant, E-7.

H-34. A Sikorsky medium helicopter used by the Marines in the earliest years of the Vietnam War.

Han tu. Vietnamese for "blood debt." It can also mean revenge or hatred.

H-hour. The hour at which an operation, usually an amphibious landing, is to begin.

HMM. Abbreviation for Marine Medium Helicopter Squadron.

Hootch. American slang for Vietnamese house.

HQ. Headquarters.

Huey. Generic term for what the U.S. Army called the Bell HU-1E Iroquois and the Marines called the UH-1E helicopter. A light-attack and passenger helicopter.

III MAF. III Marine Amphibious Force. At the time of Starlite it was commanded by LtGen Lewis W. Walt.

JATO. For jet-assisted takeoff. Rockets attached to the wings of aircraft to permit them to take off on short runways.

KC-130. The primary Marine cargo and air-refueling aircraft.

KIA. Killed in action.

L-hour. For landing hour. The hour at which a helicopter landing operation is to begin.

Lance Corporal (LCpl). The third lowest enlisted Marine rank. It is above private first class and below corporal.

LCM. Landing Craft, Medium

Light Antiaircraft Missile (LAAM) Battalion. Marine air-defense battalions armed with the HAWK ground-to-air missiles.

LSD. Landing Ship Dock. Amphibious ship that transports amtracs to the objective area.

LST. Landing Ship Tank. Flat-bottomed, ocean-going vessel capable of hauling troops, tanks, and other heavy equipment.

Lt. Leiutenant.

LtCol. Lieutenant colonel.

LtGen. Lieutenant general.

LZ. Landing zone for helicopters.

M14. The 7.62mm (.30-caliber) service rifle for the Marines at the time of Starlite. An updated version of the M1 rifle of World War II fame, it had a short life. It was phased in in 1962 and phased out in favor of the 5.52mm (.223-caliber) M-16 in 1967.

M48. Main U.S. battle tank during the Vietnam War.

M60. The 7.62mm machine gun used by the Marines and U.S. Army in Vietnam.

M79. The 40mm grenade launcher used by the U.S. and ARVN.

Maj. Major.

MajGen. Major general.

Marine Air Group. The intermediate Marine air unit, commanded by a colonel. It normally had three or more squadrons attached.

Marine Raiders. Elite Marine units during World War II. They were phased out early in the war.

Master Sergeant (MSgt). Pay grade E-8, the second highest pay grade for an enlisted man. Although this is the same pay grade as a first sergeant, it means that the holder of the rank is in a technical field, e.g. electronics, or administration, rather than in the command functions.

Medal of Honor. America's highest military decoration for valor. Very often incorrectly called the Congressional Medal of Honor.

Medevac. Medical evacuation.

MP. Military Police.

Navy Cross Medal. America's second highest military valor decoration for Marines and Navy personnel.

Ontos. Greek for "the thing," this was a lightly-armored, tracked-vehicle that sported six 106mm recoilless rifles.

Pfc. Private first class.

Popular Forces. A type of South Vietnamese local militia.

Purple Heart. America's oldest military decoration, it designates that the holder has been wounded in action against an armed enemy.

Republic of Vietnam. South Vietnam. Our allies in the war.

RLT. Regimental landing team. Made up of two or more infantry battalions and support units.

RPG. Rocket-propelled grenade. Manufactured in the Soviet Union or China, these were easily transportable, anti-bunker and anti-armor weapons.

S-1. A unit's personnel and administration officer.

S-2. A unit's intelligence officer.

S-3. A unit's operations officer.

S-4. A unit's logistics officer.

Sapper. Western term for infiltrator and saboteur. The Vietnamese called these men "special forces."

SATS. Short airfield for tactical support. An expeditionary airfield designed to be rapidly constructed by Marines or Seabees in a combat environment.

Sgt. Sergeant, E-5.

Silver Star Medal. America's third highest military valor decoration.

SNCO. Staff non-commissioned officer. Pay grades E-6 to E-9.

Spider hole. Small, camouflaged, one-man fighting hole.

SSgt. Staff Sergeant, E-6.

TAOR. Tactical area of responsibility. A unit's area of operations.

Tonkin Gulf incidents. Two clashes in the Tonkin Gulf between U.S. Navy and North Vietnamese naval forces. What actually happened is still in dispute. The Johnson administration used these incidents as an excuse to begin bombing North Vietnam. Congress also passed the so-called Tonkin Gulf Resolution that gave the President expanded powers in dealing with North Vietnam.

USA. United States Army.

USAF. United States Air Force.

USMC. United States Marine Corps.

USN. United States Navy.

USS. United States ship.

Viet Minh. The designation of the Vietnamese communist armed forces that fought the French.

Vietnamese Cross of Gallantry. A military valor decoration presented to members of the South Vietnamese and U.S. Military by the Republic of Vietnam.

VMA. Marine Attack squadron. At the time of Starlite, they flew the A-4 Skyhawk.

VMF/A. Marine Fighter/Attack squadron. At the time of Starlite, they flew the F4 Phantom.

VMO. Marine Observation squadron.

VNMC. Vietnamese Marine Corps.

Wermacht. German military forces in World War II.

WIA. Wounded in Action.

XO. Executive officer. Second-in-command of a military tactical unit (company through regiment).

ACKNOWLEDGEMENTS

I was able to compile this book only through the cooperation of dozens of former Marines and Navy corpsmen who participated in Operation Starlite. The Vietnamese who were there made this an unusual work and I am grateful for their perspective. For the participants of both sides, recollecting these long-ago events was sometimes a painful task. I thank them for the courage they displayed in seeing it through.

Thanks also to the archivists, the keepers of the records. Without them, much of what I heard from the participants, whose memories were decades old and embedded in the fog of war, could not have been sorted out. Particularly helpful were Kerry Strong, director of the U.S. Marine Corps University Archives, and Clifford Snyder, military archivist at the National Archives. A special thanks goes to my friend Col John Ripley, USMC (Retired), director of the History and Museums Division, Headquarters Marine Corps, and his staff. I am also grateful to Susan Hodges of the Marine Corps Heritage Foundation, and to the Foundation itself for approving a grant that enabled me to travel to the Washington area to put the finishing touches on the manuscript. Ed "Coconut Ensemble" Henry of Military Historical

Tours, in Alexandria, Virginia, provided me with the contacts I needed to interview to former Viet Cong and shared his wealth of knowledge about our former enemy. Ed and Professor Alexander "Sandy" Cochran of the National War College, retired Marines Capt Ed Garr and MGySgt Ron Keene, and former Marines Bill Douglass and Fred Caron also read early drafts of the manuscript and made many valuable suggestions. I could not have interviewed the Bo Doi without the impressive skills of Vo Duc Tam, professor of English at Hue University. Thanks, Tam. I am grateful for the patience of Col Mike Harrington, USMCR (Ret), who is not a lawyer after all. Finally, and especially, the warmest of thanks to Susy King, whose help in getting the grunt work done was an effort from the heart.

NOTES

CHAPTER 1

1. Cable of February 27, 1946 from Kenneth Landon, Reported in Herring, George C., ed. *The Pentagon Papers,* Abridged Edition. New York: McGraw-Hill, 1993, p. 4. Hereafter, *Pentagon Papers.*

2. Stetler, Russell. ed. *The Military Art of People's War: Selected Writings of Vo Nguyen Giap,* Hereafter Stetler, New York: Monthly Review Press, 1970, p. 50. The Viet Minh was a shortened version of *Viet Minh Doc Lap Dong Minh Hoi* (Vietnam Independence League).

3. McNamara, Robert S., with Brian VanDerMark. *In Retrospect: the Tragedy and Lessons of Vietnam,* New York: Times Books, 1995, pp. 83-85.

4. Sorley, Lewis, *Honorable Warrior: General Harold K. Johnson and the Ethics of Command,* Lawrence, KS: University Press of Kansas, 1998, p. 153.

5. Ibid., p. 225.

6. Ibid., p. 157.

7. Pike, Douglas *PAVN: People's Army of Vietnam,* Novato, CA: Presidio Press, 1986, p. 9.

8. Ibid.

9. Nguyen Khac Vien. *Vietnam: a Long History,* (rev) Hanoi: Gioi Publishers, 1993, pp. 20-29. Hereafter Nguyen.

10. Boettcher, Thomas D. *Vietnam, The Valor and the Sorrow, From the Home Front to the Front Lines in Words and Pictures.* Boston: Little Brown, 1985, pp. 8. Hereafter Boettcher.

11. Patti, Archimedes L.A. *Why Vietnam? Prelude to America's Albatross,* Berkeley: University of California Press, 1980, p. 132. Patti was an OSS officer who was parachuted into Vietnam during World War II to assist the Vietnamese against the Japanese.

12. Boettcher, pp. 13-15.

13. Boettcher, pp. 13-29.

14. Ho Chi Minh's background has in many cases been blurred by the hagiographic efforts of his admirers. Even his critics have had a hard time uncovering the truth of his early years. Ho was unusually secretive, even for a revolutionary, and the whole story may never be told. The cited material is from Boettcher, pp. 71-78.

15. Currey, Cecil B. *Victory at any Cost: The Genius of Vietnam's Vo Nguyen Giap,* Hereafter, Curry, Washington, DC: Brassey's, 1997, pp. 22-23.

16. Ibid., pp. 42-43.

17. Boettcher, pp. 51-52.

18. Ibid., pp. 84-85.

19. Ibid. pp. 55-57.

20. Stetler, p. 57.

21. Attributed to General Lyman L. Lemnitzer, Chairman of the Joint Chiefs of Staff.

22. Nguyen, p. 30.

CHAPTER 2

1. Dallek, Robert. *Flawed Giant, Lyndon B. Johnson, 1960-1973,* New York: Oxford University Press, 1998.

2. Shultz, Richard H. Jr. *The Secret War Against Hanoi: Kennedy's and Johnson's Use of Spies, Saboteurs, and Covert Warriors in North Vietnam,* New York: Harper Collins, 1999, p. 191. Hereafter Shultz.

3. Tonkin Gulf Resolution. House and Senate Joint Resolution, August 7, 1964. Washington, DC: Department of State Bulletin, August 29, 1964, p. 268.

4. Ford, Harold P. *CIA and the Vietnam Policy Makers: Three Episodes 1962-1968*, Hereafter Ford, Washington, DC: CIA Center for the Study of Intelligence, 1998, online edition, p. 7.

5. Ibid., p. 17.

6. Ibid., p. 22.

7. Currey, p. 245, note 1.

8. Shulimson, Jack, and Major Charles M. Johnson, USMC. *U.S. Marines in Vietnam: The Landing and the Buildup, 1965*, Washington, DC, U.S. Government Printing Office, 1978, p. 7. Hereafter, Shulimson.

9. JCS msg to CinCPac, dated March 6, 1965, quoted in Shulimson, p. 16.

10. Beschloss, Michael. *Reaching for Glory: Lyndon Johnson's Secret White House Tapes, 1964-1965.* New York: Simon and Shuster, 2001, pp. 214-15.

11. Ibid., p. 194.

12. *Pentagon Papers*, pp. 115-16.

13. Author interviews with the Bo Doi, the Viet Cong "Freedom Fighters," September 1999.

14. Pentagon Papers, pp. 120-21

15. Summers, Harry G. Jr. *On Strategy: A Critical Analysis of the Vietnam War.* Novato, CA: Presidio Press, 1982, p. 92

CHAPTER 3

1. Unless otherwise indicated, information for this chapter came from interviews with former members of 3d Battalion, 3d Marines, and 2d Battalion, 4th Marines.

2. McCutcheon, LtGen Keith B., USMC, "Marine Aviation in Vietnam 1962-1970" in U.S. Government Printing Office, *The Marines in Vietnam, 1954-1773: An Anthology and Annotated Bibliography*, 2d ed. Washington, DC 1985, pp. 266-68. Unless otherwise indicated, all information about the construction of the Chulai airstrip came from this source.

3. Conversation between the author and General Charles C. Krulak, USMC, son of Victor Krulak, July 1998.

4. *Stars and Stripes,* article, probably dated in July 1965. The author has the clipping but not the complete citation, which includes date.

5. Harry Reasoner, ABC Evening News, February 10, 1971

6. The information about VMA-225 came from correspondence between the author and former VMA-225 pilot Jules Townsend in 1992-1993.

7. Ibid.

8. Ibid.

9. Ibid.

CHAPTER 4

1. Schell, Jonathan. "The Military Half: An Account of the Destruction in Quang Ngai and Quang Tin," in *Reporting Vietnam, Part One: American Journalism 1959-1969*. New York: The American Library, pp. 389-391.

2. Unless otherwise indicated, all information about the 1st VC, or Ba Gia, Regiment was obtained through a series of interviews with the Bo Doi, former members of the regiment, in September 1999.

3. Sources vary widely regarding the number of landowners and "rich" peasants who were executed during this reform. The numbers range from a low of 10,000 to a high of 100,000. In any event, Ho Chi Minh publicly announced that they had been overzealous in this project and made "many mistakes."

4. Shultz, pp. 84-90.

5. Corson, William R. *The Betrayal*. New York: Norton, 1968, pp. 140-142.

6. Taylor, Sandra C. Vietnamese *Women at War: Fighting for Ho Chi Minh and Revolution.,* Lawrence, KS: University Press of Kansas, 1999. This is an account of the role of women in the war.

7. Olson, James S. and Randy Roberts. *Where the Domino Fell: America and Vietnam 1945 to 1990.* New York: St. Martins, 1991, pp. 67-68.

8. 1st *Construction Site*, the code name and original designation of the 1st VC Regiment, is the literal translation of the Vietnamese term *Cong-truong*.

9. Currey, pp. 83.

10. USMACV Log No. 6-59-65, translation of a document captured on May 31, 1965, after the first battle of Ba Gia.

11. Interrogation SIC Report 171/65 dated August 27, 1965.

12. USMACV Interrogation Report, Log Number 9-161-65, Control No. 180665, dated September 24, 1965.

13. USMACV, J3, Daily Staff Journal, May 29-31, 1965.

14. Ibid.

15. Ibid.

16. Ibid.

17. Shulimson, p. 51.

18. USMACV Interrogation Report, Log Number 9-161-65, Control No. 180665, dated September 24, 1965.

19. USMACV Interrogation Report, Log No. 9-406-56, Control No. 1807-65, undated.

20. Ibid.

21. Ibid.

22. Pamphlet published by the Veteran's Liaison Committee, Ba Gia Regiment, Military Region V, undated and furnished the author by one of the Bo Doi, Colonel Tran Nhu Tiep.

23. USMACV, J3, Daily Staff Journal, July 5-7, 1965.

24. USMACV Interrogation Report, Log Number 9-161-65, Control No. 180665, dated September 24, 1965.

25. Lanning, Michael Lee and Dan Cragg. *Inside the VC and NVA: The Real Story of North Vietnam's Armed Forces.* New York: Fawcett Columbine, 1992, pp. 94-95.

26. USMACV J2 Log. No. 9-205-65 dated July 3, 1965.

CHAPTER 5

1. Shulimson, p. 69. According to Colonel Charles Williamson, USMC (Retired), the intelligence was actually gathered by the Intelligence (G-2) staff of the 3d Marine Division but was appropriated by the staff of its parent unit, the III Marine Amphibious Force which claimed it as its own. Interview between the author and Colonel Williamson, March 2001.

2. 4th Marines Command Chronology, August 1965.

3. USMACV Interrogation Report Log No. 9-161-65, Control No. 180665, dated September 24, 1965.

4. Shulimson, p. 70.

5. Ibid.

6. Tape of MajGen Oscar F. Peatross, USMC. Oral History Collection, Headquarters U.S. Marine Corps, Division of History and Museums. Hereafter Peatross.

7. Ibid.

8. Shulimson, p. 70.

9. Peatross.

10. Data on Peatross from History and Museums Division, Headquarters, U.S. Marine Corps, file on MajGen Oscar F. Peatross and Blankfort, Michael, *The Big Yankee: the Story of Evans Carlson and the Raiders.* Boston: Little Brown, 1947.

11. Peatross.

12. Ibid.

13. Peatross, Oscar F., "Victory at Van Tuong: An Application of Doctrine," U.S. Naval Institute *Proceedings,* September 1967.

14. Peatross.

15. Shulimson, p. 72.

16. Peatross comments on Shulimson draft manuscript, dtd 7Jun71.

17. Shulimson, pp. 70-71.

18. Fall, Bernard B. *Street Without Joy* Mechanicsburg, PA: Stackpole, 1961, p. 78.

19. Shulimson.

20. Shulimson, p. 72.

21. Ibid.

22. Logbooks from USS *Bayfield, Cabildo,* and *Vernon County,* 17-18 August 1965.

23. Currey, p. 56. When the Chinese Communists standardized their equipment along Russian lines after the Korean War they sent most of the U.S.-made weaponry captured from the Kuomintang and the South Koreans to the North Vietnamese. The Viet Cong augmented this with equipment captured from the ARVN.

CHAPTER 13

1. Shulimson, p. 87

2. Teller, Maj Gary L., LtCol Lane Rogers, and Keith V. Fleming, Jr. *U.S. Marines in Vietnam: Fighting the North Vietnamese, 1967.* Washington, DC: History and Museums Division, Headquarters, Marine Corps, 1984, p. 119.

3. "Van-Tuong, A Glorious. Victory (Van Tuong—Mot Chien Cong Oanh Liet)." This is a chapter from a book written by one of the Bo Doi, Col Tran Nhu Tiep. He refused to let me have a copy of the entire book, saying that it was still classified material. He did, however, copy several pages for my use.

CHAPTER 14

1. Arnold, Hugh M. "Official Justifications for America's Role in Indochina" *Asian Affairs*, Sep/Oct 1975, p. 31.

2. Lewy, Gunter. *America in Vietnam*: New York: Oxford University Press, 1978, pp. 446-447.

3. Olson and Robert, *Where the Domino* Fell, p. 70.

4. Summers, Harry G., Jr., *On Strategy: A Critical Analysis of the Vietnam War*, Novato, CA: Presidio Press, 1982. p.68.

5. This manual has been reprinted several times and the Marines are using it in Iraq.

6. Ford, p. 1.

7. Shulimson, Jack. *U.S. Marines in Vietnam: an Expanding War*, 1966, Washington, DC: U.S. Government Printing Office, 1982, p. 44.

8. USMACV letter to CG III MAF dtd July 4, 1966. Subj: Military Support for Revolutionary Development, encl. 9, 3dMarDiv Command Chronology, July 66. Quoted in Shulimson, Jack. *U.S. Marines in Vietnam: an Expanding War*, 1966, Washington, DC: U.S. Government Printing Office, 1982, p. 233.

9. Clausewitz, Carl von. *On War*, Indexed Edition, Princeton: Princeton University Press, 1984, I:1, p. 80.

10. The World Bank.

11. Reuters News Agency, reported on CNN online March 18, 2000.

BIBLIOGRAPHY

BOOKS:

Beschloss, Michael. *Reaching for Glory: Lyndon Johnson Secret White House Tapes, 1964-1965*. New York: Simon and Shuster, 2001.

Blankfort, Michael. *The Big Yankee: the Story of Evans Carlson and the Raiders*. Boston: Little Brown, 1947.

Boettcher, Thomas D. *Vietnam. The Valor and the Sorrow, From the Home Front to the Front Lines in Words and Pictures*. Boston: Little Brown, 1985.

Clausewitz, Carl von. *On War*, Indexed Edition, Princeton: Princeton University Press, 1984.

Corson, William R. *The Betrayal*. New York: Norton, 1968.

Currey, Cecil B. *Victory at any Cost: The Genius of Vietnam Vo Nguyen Giap*. Washington, DC: Brassey, 1997.

Dallek, Robert. *Flawed Giant, Lyndon B. Johnson, 1960-1973*. New York: Oxford University Press, 1998.

Fall, Bernard B. *Street Without Joy*. Mechanicsburg, PA: Stackpole, 1961.

Ford, Harold P. *CIA and the Vietnam Policy Makers: Three Episodes 1962-1968*. Washington, DC: CIA Center for the Study of Intelligence, 1998.

Herring, George C. ed. *The Pentagon Papers* Abridged Edition. New York: McGraw-Hill, 1993.

Lanning, Michael Lee, and Dan Cragg. *Inside the VC and NVA: The Real Story of North Vietnam Armed Forces.* New York: Fawcett Columbine, 1992.

Lewy, Gunter. *America in Vietnam:* New York: Oxford University Press, 1978.

Lind, Michael. *Vietnam: The Necessary War: A Reinterpretation of America Most Disastrous Military Conflict.* New York: Free Press, 1999.

McNamara, Robert S., with Brian VanDerMark. *In Retrospect: the Tragedy and Lessons of Vietnam.* New York: Times Books, 1995.

Nguyen Khac Vien. *Vietnam: a Long History.* (rev) Hanoi: Gioi Publishers, 1993.

Patti, Archimedes L.A. *Why Vietnam? Prelude to America Albatross.* Berkeley: University of California Press, 1980.

Olson, James S. and Randy Roberts. *Where the Domino Fell: America and Vietnam 1945 to 1990.* New York: St. Martins, 1991.

Pike, Douglas. *PAVN: People's Army of Vietnam.* Novato, CA: Presidio Press, 1986.

Sorley, Lewis. *Honorable Warrior: General Harold K. Johnson and the Ethics of Command.* Lawrence, KS: University Press of Kansas, 1998.

Stetler, Russell. ed. *The Military Art of People War: Selected Writings of Vo Nguyen Giap.* New York: Monthly Review Press, 1970.

Shulimson, Jack. *U.S. Marines in Vietnam: an Expanding War*, 1966. Washington, DC: U.S. Government Printing Office, 1982.

Shulimson, Jack, and Maj Charles M. Johnson, USMC. *U.S. Marines in Vietnam: The Landing and the Buildup, 1965.* Washington, DC, U.S. Government Printing Office, 1978.

Shultz, Richard H. Jr. *The Secret War Against Hanoi: Kennedy and Johnson Use of Spies, Saboteurs, and Covert Warriors in North Vietnam.* New York: Harper Collins, 1999.

Summers, Harry G., Jr. *On Strategy: A Critical Analysis of the Vietnam War.* Novato, CA: Presidio Press, 1982.

Taylor, Sandra C. *Vietnamese Women at War: Fighting for Ho Chi Minh and Revolution.* Lawrence, KS: University Press of Kansas, 1999.

Teller, Maj Gary L., USMC, LtCol Lane Rogers, USMC, and V. Keith Fleming, Jr. *U.S. Marines in Vietnam: Fighting the North Vietnamese, 1967.* Washington, DC: History and Museums Division, Headquarters, Marine Corps, 1984.

ARTICLES

Arnold, Hugh M. "Official Justifications for Americ's Role in Indochina," *Asian Affairs*, Sep/Oct 1975.

McCutcheon, LtGen Keith B., USMC, "Marine Aviation in Vietnam 1962-1970," *The Marines in Vietnam, 1954-1773: An Anthology and Annotated Bibliography*, 2d ed. U.S. Government Printing Office: Washington, DC, 1985.

Peatross, Oscar F., "Victory at Van Tuong: An Application of Doctrine," Annapolis, MD: U.S. Naval Institute *Proceedings*, September 1967.

Schell, Jonathan. "The Military Half: An Account of the Destruction in Quang Ngai and Quang Tin," *Reporting Vietnam, Part One: American Journalism 1959-1969*. New York: The American Library, 1998.

Tran Nhu, Col Tiep, Vietnamese Army. "Van Tuong—Mot Chien Cong Oanh Liet," ("Van-Tuong, A Glorious Victory"). Title and publishing data of book unknown.

OTHER SOURCES

3d Battalion, 3d Marines Command Chronology, August 1965. USMC Historical Center.

4th Marines Command Chronology, August 1965. USMC Historical Center.

7th Marines Command Chronology, August 1965. USMC Historical Center.

History and Museums Division, Headquarters U.S. Marine Corps, Washington, DC. Oral History Collection. Tape of MajGen Oscar F. Peatross.

History and Museums Division, Headquarters, U.S. Marine Corps, Washington, DC. File on MajGen Oscar F. Peatross.

Naval Historical Center, Washington, DC. Logbooks from USS *Bayfield,* USS *Cabildo,* and USS *Vernon County,* August 17-18, 1965.

U.S. Department of State Bulletin. House and Senate Joint Resolution of August 7, 1964. onkin Gulf Resolution. Washington, DC: Bulletin, August 29, 1964.

USMACV Log No. June 29, 1965. National Archives, College Park, MD.

USMACV Interrogation SIC Report 171/65 August 27, 1965. National Archives, College Park, MD.

USMACV Interrogation Report, Log Number 9-161-65, Control No. 180665. September 24, 1965. National Archives, College Park, MD.

USMACV, J3, Daily Staff Journal, May 29-31, 1965 National Archives, College Park, MD.

USMACV Interrogation Report, Log Number 9-161-65, Control No. 180665. September 24, 1965. National Archives, College Park, MD.

USMACV Interrogation Report, Log No. 9-406-56, Control No. 1807-65, undated. National Archives, College Park, MD.

Veteran Liaison Committee, Ba Gia Regiment, Military Region V, Pamphlet. National Archives, College Park, MD.

USMACV, J3, Daily Staff Journal, July 5-7, 1965. National Archives, College Park, MD.

USMACV Interrogation Report, Log Number 9-161-65, Control No. 180665. September 24, 1965. National Archives, College Park, MD.

USMACV J2 Log. No. 9-205-65. July 3, 1965. National Archives, College Park, MD.

USMACV Interrogation Report Log No. 9-161-65, Control No. 180665, September 24, 1965. National Archives, College Park, MD.

INDEX